HAVING YOUR ALL

How self-care leads to an **Energized, Empowered** and **Effective** life

EMMA FOGT | NISHA SHAH
MBA, MS, RDN | MPH, RDN

e WOMENWELLNESS®

Copyright 2014

Published and distributed in the United States by eWomenWellness®

All rights reserved. No part of this book may be reproduced by any mechanical, photographic or electronic process, or in the form of a phonographic recording; nor may it be stored in a retrieval system, transmitted or otherwise be copied for public or private use-other than for "fair use" as brief quotations embodies in articles and reviews- without prior written permission of the publisher.

Although every effort has been made to provide accurate and up-to-date information, this document cannot be guaranteed to be free of factual error. All of the recommendations set forth in these pages are supported by research; many are based on observational studies. Observational studies are not the gold standard of research known as randomized clinical trials, so although the cause and effect cannot be definitively established, in many instances the association and potential health benefits can be.

The authors of this book do not dispense medical advice or prescribe the use of any techniques as a form of treatment for physical, emotional, or medical problems without the advice of a physician, either directly or indirectly. The intent of the authors is only to offer information of a general nature to help you in your quest for emotional and spiritual wellbeing. In the event that you use any of the information in this book for yourself, which is your constitutional right, the author and publisher assume no responsibility for your actions.

Tradepaper ISBN: 978-0-9899785-0-7
Digital ISBN: 978-0-9899785-1-4
Library of Congress Number: 2014930077

1st Edition January 2014
Printed on demand in the United States of America

DEDICATION

To my aunt, Manjula.
Her courage, passion, and vision of life
have been my inspiration
since I was a little girl sleeping with
her books stacked around me in bed.
~ Nisha

To my parents,
Dr. George P. and Daphne M. Lewis,
for sharing the best of the sciences and arts
with their four girls.
~ Emma

*Take care of your body.
It's the only place you have to live.*

JIM ROHN

TABLE OF CONTENTS

Acknowlegements	9
Introduction	11
Part 1: The Full-Plate Syndrome™	15
Chapter 1-Having IT All—Redefined	17
Chapter 2-How Did We Get Here In The First Place?	23
Chapter 3- The "Exhausted" Woman	31
Part 2: Struggling With The Juggling	37
Chapter 4- Should We Lean In, Lean Out, Or Just Stay In Bed?	39
Chapter 5-Stress 9-5 And Beyond	45
Chapter 6-The "Evolved" Woman	55
Part 3: Having "Your" All	61
Chapter 7-Define Your Values/Define Your Success	63
Chapter 8-Living With Passion	69
Chapter 9-Choose Happy	73
Part 4: You First!	77
Chapter 10-Success Through Self-Care	79
Chapter 11-No More Excuses	85
Chapter 12-Get Your Groove On	95
Chapter 13- Get Ready, Mind Set, Go!	103
Part 5: The 5 Power Habits	107
Chapter 14- It's Time To Power Up!	109
Power Habit #1: Purpose	115

Scratching The Itch
Finding Flow
Discover Joy In Every Day
Get Creative
Authentic Self
Don't "Should" On Yourself
The Secrets Of Happy Women
Attitude Of Gratitude
Maintain Curiosity
Build Your Personal Power

Power Habit #2: Balance — 137
The Present Of Presence
Take Back Your Time
Tame The Monkey Mind
Get Organized
Simplify, Simplify, Simplify
Stress-Free Living
Live In Moderation
Face Time
No Hocus Pocus In Focus
The Balance Leader

Power Habit #3: Rejuvenation — 159
Sleep Is Not A Luxury
It's Playtime!
Get Away/Retreats
Get Unplugged
Energy Boosters
Laugh, Giggle, Smile
Read This
Get Outside
Small Fixes For Big Results
Make A Style Statement

Power Habit #4: Move — 181
Make Moving Fun
Mind-Body Activities
Stand Up Straight
Be Strong
Fitting Fitness In
Metabolism Boosters
Walk This Way
Flexibility & Balance
Partner Up
Nature's Calling

Power Habit #5: Nourish — 203
Super Food Multi-Taskers
Energize Your Day
Think Your Drink
Mindful Eating
The Nutrition Essentials
Carb Conundrum
Weight Management
Eating On The Go
Eat Clean
Go Green

Conclusion — 225

Notes: References & Bibliography — 227

Biographies — 242
Emma Fogt MBA, MS, RDN, FAND
Nisha Shah MPH, RDN

ACKNOWLEDGEMENTS

We would like to thank all of the incredible people in our lives who supported us in making this book come to life:

- **Thank you** to our husbands for putting up with our numerous late nights at the computer; for listening, discussing, and reviewing information on women's issues; for picking up the slack when we were trying to meet our deadlines; and for believing in and supporting us in our vision.

- **Thank you** to our editor, Dawn Josephson, for helping us find our writing voices and moving us from ideas to a finished project much faster and with more fun than what we could have done on our own.

- **Thank you** to our designer extraordinaire, Summer Morris, whose talent helped us put a face to our vision and gave us a finished product we could be so proud of.

- **Thank you** to all the women who took their time to share their stories with us in our interviews … you know who you are! Your support to this project was invaluable, and so much of your wisdom can be found in this book.

- **Thank you** to all of the girlfriends, sisters, walking and book club buddies, tennis partners, fellow nutrition entrepreneurs, and colleagues in our lives who have stood by us in all those moments when we weren't feeling like we were having much of anything! Your support, inspiration, encouragement, and wonderful discussions helped us reach this point. We are truly grateful to have you in our lives!

- **Thank you** to our amazing mothers, aunts, grandmothers, role models, and mentors for paving the way for the freedom and opportunities the two of us have in our lives today. Your generation pushed the boundaries and expanded women's roles to a place where the desire to write a book can so easily turn into a reality. We owe so much to you.

- **Thank you** to our two sons for being part of a male gender that doesn't believe in stereotypical roles and who are willing to be part of the solution to the challenges of juggling all of the responsibilities in life today.

- **Thank you** to our two daughters who are our secret motivations for writing this book. We hope our words contribute to opening the doors to prioritizing balance, self-care, and well-being into your lives. We look forward to supporting you in "having your all"!

- **And a big thank you** to each other for making such a big endeavor so much more fun and exciting than doing it on our own… for all the hours of in depth and energized conversations leading to a culmination of concepts and ideas… for helping each other get through the challenges of writing a book on top of everything else we were doing in our lives… for having faith in each other and the power of what women can accomplish when they work together. And thanks for always being a friend first before being a business partner.

INTRODUCTION

It's still dark out. What time is it? 2:30am? What should I wear for the media shoot? Will I make the dentist appointment on time in between clients? Did I get that school permission slip signed? These thoughts and more are milling through my head as I fretfully try to go back to sleep. Better get up and read. No, maybe I should check e-mails. What am I thinking? No one is e-mailing at 3am ... unless they are in China. I wonder what people are doing in China right now?

By the time I fall back to sleep, it feels like it's time to get up because it is... I overslept! I grab the food props I prepped last night for the live TV segment on Favorite Fall Foods: baked apple and roasted vegetables all packed in their neat containers. I remember to pull out my son's lunch from the fridge and place it on the kitchen table. I arrive at the set and place the container holding the baked apple on the table. As I flip open the lid, instead of that beautiful honey baked apple, inside the container is my son's lunch!

It's 3:55pm and I'm driving as safely as I can for a mad woman who's going to be late to pick her daughter up from the bus stop on a rainy day. Maybe the bus will be late. Who am I kidding? It's never as late as I tend to be coming from work. I pull up and there is my little one looking like a wet puppy. No time to wallow in my guilt, as I now have to hurry up and get her to her sport's practice.

HAVING YOUR ALL

After digging around the car for that box of granola bars I put in the car last week for snacks, I have her change into her sport gear in the back seat of the car. Darn, only one bar left! I hear my stomach grumble and I wish I would have brought some healthy snacks for both of us. As we pull up to the practice, my scheduled conference call comes in and I begin my specialized hand signals that I communicate with the kids when I'm on work calls. Out she goes and out comes my portable work station—the phone on speaker, my computer in my lap, and note taking from the dashboard. Need to shift gears, but I'm hungry, frazzled, and I just realized that I need to pee!

Who would have thought that a chance meeting and a brief business card exchange at a nutrition conference in San Diego would lead to the creation of this book and global leadership program? That is exactly how the two of us met and began working together to develop *Having Your All*.

We connected because we had one thing in common—we both were passionate about developing a platform where our skills, knowledge, and experience could make a difference in the lives of our fellow "girlfriends in distress." We understand the unique challenges and stressors women face in the workforce today and were motivated to share the strategies and tools we have found success with in our work. Our message, however, is not just for women—we invite men to utilize the concepts within this book as well. Defining your personal version of success and prioritizing self-care is a universal message and a need that crosses gender lines.

Since our initial nutrition training in the 1980s and early 90s, we have promoted health and wellness to others in just about every kind of setting: hospitals, universities, in clinical research, private practice, weight management programs, executive health, non-profits, with athletes, and in the corporate arena. In all those settings, we were exposed to a wide variety of client personalities and varying degrees of motivation to make lifestyle changes. Yet, in our combined 45 plus years as health experts, we have seen that no matter how many fruits and vegetables you eat, no

Introduction

matter how many yoga classes you take, and no matter how many stress reduction seminars you have attended, you still have to practice self-care each and every day in order to protect your greatest asset—yourself.

As working women and mothers, we are no strangers to the effects that stress and juggling too much in our work and in life has on our health and well-being. In fact, those descriptions that start this book are not from our clients, but from our own personal stories. We have experienced our own physical and emotional breakdowns as a result of pushing ourselves too hard and taking too much onto our plates. We also feel the pressure women face to overachieve in our society and be everything to everyone. So why write a book that makes the statement that as women you can "have your all"?

- We believe that "having your all" trumps "having it all."
- We believe that once women define for themselves what success means to them, they are better able to achieve a more balanced and meaningful life.
- We believe that making self-care a priority is essential for women to be able to go after what they want in life, be strong leaders, and sustain optimal health and well-being.
- We believe that our generation of women can be role models to positively influence society, our home lives, workplaces, and the next generation of girls to lead an energized, empowered, and effective life.
- We believe that no matter what profession or socioeconomic status, all women deserve to maintain their well-being and prioritize self-care.
- Finally, we believe that you can have "your" all when you are able to care for yourself on your own terms, completely designed and suited to meet your lifestyle and personal preferences.

We look forward to helping you lead *energized, empowered, and effective* lives … *Welcome to Having Your All!*

PART I

The Full-Plate Syndrome™

CHAPTER ONE

Having It All – Redefined

Imagine a fictionalized reality show that exaggerates the game of life. Instead of, *So, You Think You Can Dance*, the name of the show is changed to *So, You Think You Can Have It All?* In this game show, women compete to see who can juggle the most responsibilities in their busy lives to determine who is the most "successful" woman of them all. The women try to one-up each other in this elimination-style competition where the bar is raised every week.

You had the most volunteer hours at work? Well, I'm going to run for PTA president. You get in five sessions of yoga per week? Well, I belong to three book clubs. You are going to double income figures for the month? Well, I'm going to start a non-profit organization to save the rain forests in South America ... all in high heels!

At the end, the winner gets a gold trophy and a week at a spa resort because she is going to need it to mentally and physically recover. What do you think? Ready to sign up?

This all may be a little tongue-in-cheek, but isn't this what women tend to do with their lives? We have stopped thinking about what we really want and instead keep looking around at what other women and men are doing with their work and personal lives. We sign-up, volunteer, and accept projects to prove that we can handle it all while filling up our already overloaded plates. If having a lot on our plates means we are important and successful, then we can play that game. Take on the new client based in Shanghai? Sure! Serve as the charity gala chair? What an honor! Sell Girl Scout cookies with the troop this weekend? Wouldn't miss it! Play on the work softball team? You bet!

But the real question is ... do we *really want* to do any of these things? Are we saying yes simply because we think we should? Or maybe because someone we know is doing these things, so therefore we think we need to, as well? Is that the kind of "having it all" women today really want—commitments, responsibilities, and obligations to things that we potentially find meaningless and unfulfilling? Ultimately, the pursuit of all these endless tasks and to-do's fills up our lives, takes away our energy, and leaves us tired, cranky, and overwhelmed. At some point, something will give and it's probably what is missing the most from our plates—our sanity and our health!

So, why are we writing this book? We want to tell women today that "having it all" might just be a myth—an elusive, media-concocted dream in the clouds that, even if momentarily achieved, is never sustained for very long. But having YOUR all is achievable ... if you clearly define what is personally fulfilling to you. And we would even argue that defining your all is absolutely necessary for women to lead balanced, healthy, and meaningful lives in today's world.

It is time for you to redefine what success means to you—not society, not the workplace, not your partner, not the media, and not your mother! It's you as an individual, your vision of success, and your hopes and dreams for a meaningful and fulfilling life that determines "your" all.

> You don't have to be everything to everyone, but you do need to be important to yourself!

We have come so far as a gender, yet we still have a ways to go because we keep getting in our own way[1]. We're looking outside of ourselves for the standards and benchmarks of a successful life and as a basis for our own self-worth. As we push ourselves hard toward this external vision of "having it all," we are destroying the two things that can help us get to where we want to go: our health and our wellbeing.

We are also writing this book to share with you what we have learned from the latest research and our many years as wellness experts, combined with our own personal experiences in seeking optimal life balance. We are providing easy to integrate and practical suggestions with our *Power Habits* in order to inspire women to make a shift in how they take care of themselves and lead their lives. We strongly believe that self-care, or habits of well-being, provide an advantage to women, and that's why they need to be a top priority in YOUR life.

When you determine what the most meaningful components in your life are and clear your plate of the rest, you are able to add back and maintain the practices that help you feel good, be healthy, and boost your self-confidence. Our goal is to inspire you to make the shift so you can feel comfortable incorporating self-care into your personal success plan. We strongly believe that maintaining your well-being is essential to success and getting the most out of life—having "your" all.

We believe women need to make a change in how they live their lives. Our busy, overcommitted lifestyle doesn't come without consequences in the form of taking a toll on our health and well being. Women seem to be unhappier, unhealthier, and more stressed than ever before. The modern woman experiences mental, physical, and emotional exhaustion caused by the chronic stressors in her life today. The pressures of work and home life can seem insurmountable. We feel burned out, drained, and overwhelmed[2].

Clearly, what women have been doing has not been working. That is why the intent of this book is to remind women to put their well-being first. As we are advised every time we buckle up on an airplane to put our own oxygen masks on first before helping others, we are advising women to start taking care of themselves first. The better you care for yourself, the better you can care for others and the more good you can do in our world. We also want you to re-evaluate how you are spending your life, your expectations, and the roles you play. How can you be more and do less? What can you do to change so you can be your most successful self?

So, why just a book for women? As women ourselves, we understand the specific needs and challenges of busy women. We are just like you, except that we are health professionals who have spent over 45 years combined, finding ways to make our clients lives healthier and more productive. Along the way, we have experimented with various strategies, scoured the research for new and innovating approaches, and learned to be practical and streamlined. We have basically figured out and have been practicing the concepts that seem to work most efficiently and effectively, and this book is our chance to share them with our "girlfriends" around the world.

Also, this book is not just for women who have the ability to make choices about their priorities or for women who have the resources to afford acts of self-care, whether with enough time or finances. We certainly recognize the challenges of providing the basic needs for simply surviving in today's world. However, no matter where you are in your life stage or your financial status, there are small steps you can take to create a better life for yourself. We hope that what we present in this book can be a universal message that benefits women across all socioeconomic, education, and racial lines.

That is exactly why we encourage you to define a successful life for you. "Your" having it all, is what ever is within your reach and desire, which allows you to make your well-being a priority. We specifically designed our *Power Habits* to offer a variety of actions to take for self-care. There is no structured and rigid plan; it's up to you to choose the self-care strategies that are most accessible, affordable, and interesting to incorporate into your life. Most of the suggestions within the *Power Habits* are free and flexible enough to fit into any woman's life. And although the book is written toward the specific needs of women, we also encourage men to apply the same strategies into their lives. In fact, we incorporate this same vision in all of our work—whether with young adults or seniors, and whether at school campuses or in the boardroom.

So let's dig right into the problem that we are providing a solution for in this book. No matter where we are in our work and personal lives, most women today have overloaded plates filled with commitments, expectations, and responsibilities—much of which they don't find meaningful and fulfilling. We use the term the "*Full Plate Syndrome*" to describe how modern women's lives have so much going on, their plates are overloaded, and they feel overwhelmed, overtired, and stressed out.

What does your life plate look like right now? Is it filled with things that are leading you to your goals and the kind of success you want? Do you have enough self-care in place to maintain your health and mental well-being? Is your plate balanced between responsibilities and joys in life? Or is it piled high and overflowing with unwanted things that have to be done, expectations that have to be met, and plans to forever make?

If we equate our lifestyle choices to their equivalence in food choices, we would find that most women are carrying around an overloaded plate filled with a lot of junk food and way too much to drink! How do you feel when you overeat or have a heavy junk food day? What happens to your health? Your productivity? Your self-esteem? Your ability to reach your goals? If you're like most women, you likely feel weighed down from the stress of it all.

Take a look at how a "full-plate" can be a metaphor of our fast-paced and overloaded lives:

- We are accustomed to getting large portions on our plates.
- We are unsure of what to take on our plates because we have stopped noticing what feels good and what doesn't.
- We have someone else determining what we should have, not have, and how much is on our plates.
- We feel miserable after consuming more than we intended to.

In the long run, the *Full-Plate Syndrome*™ in relationship to our food choices causes our health to suffer through weight gain and lifestyle diseases. In relationship to life, these same choices affect our well-being and ability to be our best selves. When you don't feel good, you don't make the best choices. When you don't make the best choices, you don't feel good. Self-care is both feeling good and making the best choices for what you want out of life.

HAVING YOUR ALL

Clearing your plate is the first step to lightening your load and making room for the things in life that energize, empower, and help you to lead an effective life. We're not encouraging you to turn your life plate upside down and dump it all to start clean, but rather we would like to see you replace the heavier "junky" commitments and obligations with healthier options—those choices that bring success and are beneficial to your well-being in the long term.

You only get 24 hours each day. Therefore, you want to manage your time and energy to get the best from those hours. Your foods need to fit on your plate and you need to feed yourself the right self-care before you can feed others. What we're telling you is no different than when our moms told us to "eat your veggies because they're good for you," or "don't eat too much junk food or you'll get sick!" Think of this book as a tool to help minimize the "junk food" in your life and to get some healthy "self-care" onto your plate.

The key is to find the right portions of food (commitments, responsibilities, and self-care) for your plate in order to feel like you're having it all without getting indigestion from overdoing it! We understand that many responsibilities are non-negotiable. You have to support yourself and your family, you have loved ones to care for, and you have a home to manage. There may be times in your life where the basics are all you can handle. You might need to say no to volunteering or to the next big work project. You might even need to set better limits in your personal life and relationships.

Listen to your body for how much you can handle—know when it's time to say no to second servings of commitments. After all, you might want to save room for dessert or exciting and new opportunities that can enrich your life. Bring back the sensory enjoyment and experience of eating and living. Our message is simple: YOU alone determine the ideal ingredients and portions for your plate and for your life.

CHAPTER TWO

How Did We Get Here In the First Place?

To better understand how we reached this place of busy lives and full plates, it's helpful to take a look at a historical perspective of where we have come from as women. Women's lives have mainly been defined by their roles and responsibilities. Whether stemming from external or self-expectations, their position in society was based on these roles and as we discover, were closely related to their self-worth and well-being[3].

In the past, women followed the societal structure men created because men were the ones who held all of the power and resources, and women had limited means of subsistence. In the 1800s, both the lower and upper class women had very little choice in their lives. The women who worked outside of the home out of necessity were the original "Superwomen" as they fulfilled the roles of being mothers, workers, and housekeepers without much support from anyone. They began work between the ages of 8 and 12 and continued working throughout their lives, taking short breaks only to give birth. Barred from well-paid work, these women were forced into a very small range of occupations such as domestic service, unskilled factory hands, agricultural laborers, and even prostitution as a means to survive[4].

By the 1840s and the start of the Industrial Revolution, a mere 10% of women held jobs outside of the home, mainly due to necessity. These jobs were mostly in factories, especially sewing factories where labor was cheaper for women and children. The other 90% remained home doing domestic chores[5]. During this era, girls received less education than boys and were restricted from universities. In the upper class, women were married-off to well-to-do husbands with one goal: to produce children. If a woman remained single or childless during these times, she was not "fulfilling her duties" and therefore did not achieve "success" in her life as their sole purpose was to marry and reproduce. If a woman was unhappy with her situation, there was almost nothing she could do about it. The church, law, customs, history, and approval from society kept women limited in their freedom and actions.

It was not until the 1900s and the First and Second World Wars that women were pulled away from domestic duties and called in to work, as their husbands, brothers and fathers went off to fight. Women were herded into factories to help sew uniforms and were sought after to manufacture bullets and ammunition. For some, full time jobs even included great responsibility like managing large farms and properties[6].

After the wars were over, the men came home and women were expected to vacate their positions and return to happy domesticity. Making room for the men to reclaim the public and business spheres, women found themselves back in the home as wives and mothers.

By the mid 20th century, staying at home became idealized through the introduction of television and mass media. Women were exposed to images of a home life that included donning glamorous clothing, having a dream-like social life, and living in a perfectly decorated and kept house. Being a perfect wife with an immaculate home and flawless appearance was encouraged in Helen B. Andelin's book *Fascinating Womanhood*[7]. The courses within this book were designed to teach women how to be happy in marriage and supported the traditional roles of women as wives and mothers[8]. After all, it was the wives who were responsible for making the marriage work. Included were sections on how to fix yourself up before your husband came home, quieting and grooming the kids, and clearing up the house. The author encouraged women to greet their man from work with a tall cool beverage, well behaved spotless children, and a haven of calm!

Perhaps in an effort to keep up with such high domestic standards, the modern 1950-60s woman started to foster the first signs of mental exhaustion[9]. Stay at home women living in the suburbs had to "keep up with the Jones's," comparing their social status to one another based on consumerism. "Tupperware Parties" became famous as coffee gatherings that encouraged the buying of plastic kitchen products—all the while raising the bar and creating expectations to be the best homemaker possible. "Every woman's dream" was not necessarily the advent of new kitchen and cleaning appliances like washing machines, refrigerators, and Hoovers as advertised by the media. Many women were beginning to feel like there had to be more to experience than babies, dishes, and husbands. They felt that their contributions to the war effort had been forgotten and they were starting to look out the window and wonder if there was more to life than playing out the role of the "perfect" mother and wife.

Women felt trapped by this "problem that has no name" as written about in Betty Freidan's iconic book *The Feminine Mystic*. She described the widespread unhappiness and frustration of the women of the 1950s and 60s and the growing discontent many women couldn't quite explain[10]. They became resentful and depressed if their role as a housewife did not match their choice to be one. It's interesting to note that the high rates of depression and anxiety women experience today is not much different than back in the 1950s[11].

Of course, not every woman stayed at home. During this time after the wars, working women made up 34% of the labor force in occupations such as secretaries, receptionists, teachers, or nurses. Once out of the house and living with more independence, these women didn't want to go back to a life of primarily domestic responsibilities and social lives centered around their husband's work. They were now skilled in trades and were developing interests outside of the home. Women had experienced economic independence, and they liked it!

As the 1960s and 70s came along, opportunities for higher education were increasingly common, as it was becoming acceptable for young women to work and live independently for a time before marrying. They moved out of their isolated households into the bustle of social movements, feminism, and the causes of the times. The Vietnam War, birth control, women's rights, and free love represented for women a time of self-expression, community, and autonomy. They were demanding full involvement in all aspects of society. This was also a time when women started to explore roles outside of the traditional teacher and administrative support positions and enter into the professions of medicine, law, and business.

By the 1980s, gender equality had taken root in our culture and some women had broken through the glass ceilings to reach the C-suites. Women were told that they could do and have anything men could. Even if they weren't getting paid the same, they now had access to previously male-only opportunities. Women of the 80s went for it all in the workplace yet were still coming home in time to serve their families dinner. Their generation went from being "Super Moms" to being "Superwomen." They took on multiple roles in order to meet household and family responsibilities while working outside the home and also pursuing personal interests.

In time, maintaining success in all these arenas started to take a toll on women's health and well-being. It was impossible to spend enough time and energy on being the perfect mother, worker, and wife. Women were beginning to experience a sense of overwhelm and loss of control that was making them prone to stress and burnout. Socioenvironmental influences had women starting to feel like they had to choose between focusing on their career or their families. Staying at home had its allure but heading into the office promised more power, prestige, and money.

Many women of this generation grew up sensing the frustration of their housewife mothers who didn't have these same opportunities and they wanted to make sure they didn't go down that same path. This sparked the separation of stay-at-home versus working women. Women who chose to stay at home felt threatened by the new experiences and successes of women in the workplace. Women who worked and hired out the care of their home and children experienced guilt for not being the one to care for the family. Women had to choose sides as there was very limited support from the workplace and from husbands to be able to balance work and home. If women wanted to work, they had to still manage, one way or another, their responsibilities in the home. Stress was on its way to becoming a significant women's health concern[12].

As we hit the end of the century and toward present day, women have been able to explore and succeed outside of the home with a new independence from their previously male and home dominated lives. They had proven their capability in the workplace and all of the higher levels of politics, business, and community.

What came with this new freedom, however, was a whole new set of contradictory messages and challenges for defining women's roles and success within them. Fewer women were getting married, and those who did waited until they were much older. The more years of schooling women had, the lower number of children they were having. The number of women choosing not to have children almost doubled to 18% compared to 10% in 1976[13]. And despite great strides in succeeding in the workplace, women were still earning less and taking on more domestic and childcare responsibilities compared to men. Take a look at the current statistics…

- Women spend 33 hours a week on childcare and domestic chores versus 17 hours per week for men[14].
- Free time for women is often fragmented or mixed with childcare, housework, or errands.
- 81 – 96% of the top leading women's jobs in 2010 were still in the traditionally female fields of teaching, nursing, office/secretarial work, childcare, and bookkeeping[15].
- In 2008, 28% of working women who were unmarried with children had incomes below the poverty line[16].

Today, women are presented with new and complicated demands in their lives. Even though modern technology has eased the burden of housework and chores, the lure of efficiency has created even more things to add on the laundry list of "to-do's," like answering e-mails, reading online, posting on social media, sharing photos, and on and on. The work day is no longer limited to 9-5 with the evenings and weekends free to care for family and the home. Women work wherever they are—whether from the soccer field or from a different time zone. They have more to do than ever before and seemingly with more urgency. As a result, women's stress levels have increased over the last 30 years across almost every demographic category[17].

Life has also become more complicated as far as all the opportunities that women have these days. The women of today grew up being told they could do anything and instead heard that they had to be everything! Take a look at all the different roles a woman of the 21st century might play in just one day:

Wife	Cheerleader	Interior decorator
Mother	Social director	Hair stylist
Employee	Housekeeper	Dog walker
Nurse	Chauffeur	Laundress
Friend	Tutor	Financial manager
Chef	Mediator	Gardener
Nutritionist	Party planner	Nanny
Personal shopper	Therapist	Elderly caregiver
Crisis manager	Volunteer	Sports coach

Whew … no wonder we have full plates!

Have women evolved to a place today that may look much different from the 1800s, but that is still defined by their roles and the expectations from society? It's an important question with a complicated answer. For our purposes, however, it's important to recognize that so much of women's frustrations and unhappiness through history stems from being defined by external influences and not being able to make the choices in life that they personally find meaningful.

Single, married, kids, no kids, big career, volunteer , single mom—no matter what the circumstances, what we have concluded is that until each woman defines her own success and has the courage to live accordingly, she will potentially live with the same "problem that has no name" as many of our female fore-bearers. Your needs, desires, and well-being must become a higher priority in your life … and in society. While history explains how we got here, it is our intentions and actions from this point on that will direct our future. No matter what your personal history, it's time to outgrow your externally defined roles, throw off the covers of the past, and live freely with success on your own terms!

CHAPTER THREE
The "Exhausted" Woman

It's very difficult for high-achieving women to accept that they may need to set limits on their desires. As stated earlier, today's working generation grew up being told we could do anything, and as a result we thought that we had to be everything! As a consequence, we expect ourselves to be energetic and efficient, and to excel in every role we embody: driven employee, supportive mentor, active community member, committed spouse, helpful friend, and of course the perfect parent with the perfect children[18]. We need to stop blaming ourselves for feeling that we fall short of where we should be, when we may be setting up a bar that is set too high.

We expect to be the "everything" woman who rises early each morning with enthusiasm to knock off e-mails and work correspondence before anyone wakes up … who dresses for success after feeding her family of four plus pet, a healthy breakfast and sending them off to school on time … who commands respect at work and uses her smarts, experience, and ability to get jobs done efficiently and successfully as she maneuvers through her to-do list … who reunites with her family at the end of the day and prepares a gourmet and healthy dinner prepared from fresh ingredients from the farmers market … who makes time to work out at the gym, help the children with their homework, and complete any lingering household chores before showering and dressing, not in fleece PJs, but in something short and lacy … and who finally heads to bed with her husband and enjoys multiple orgasms until midnight!

Is this what we expect from our lives, and more important, is this what YOU want from YOUR life? Is it our innate and deep down belief that being "everything to everybody" is both desirable and possible? This is where we see women struggle in our work. There is a part of many women that see this description of life as desirable, and they are striving to make it a reality. This desire, however, doesn't come from our values and what we truly find meaningful, but rather from what the media and external influences have been feeding us.

Take a look at an example of how Madison Avenue advertising influences how we define ourselves as women and how seductive it can be to believe in it. Remember the 1980s Enjoli commercial that sings the song *I'm a Woman?* Take a look at the lyrics:

I can put the wash on the line, feed the kids, get dressed, pass out the kisses and get to work by 5 to 9.
'Cause I'm a Woman, Enjoli!
I can bring home the Bacon! Enjoli!
Fry it up in a Pan! Enjoli!
And Never, Never, Never let you forget You're a Man!
'Cause I'm a Woman! Enjoli!

These slick ads portrayed women as powerful and decisive by day and sexual, feminine, and alluring by night. We can take on all the responsibilities our mothers handled while moving into the world our fathers held court over, all while being perky and not having a hair out of place. Someone somewhere expected this to be you and me, and we bought into it!

Not that the image is not completely desirable, but it's definitely not possible all of the time. If we believe that this is the standard to live by, we will constantly feel like a failure every time something doesn't work out as it was intended. and that certainly takes a massive toll on our health and wellbeing. We also don't do moderation very well in our society and we have taken what the media has presented to us and supersized our expectations of ourselves[19].

We might have "come along way, baby" as the Virginia Slims cigarette ads used to tell us as they marketed their campaign to young professional women, but have we really? We may have turned in our frying pan for a microwave, but the research has been clear that despite substantial gains in wages, educational attainment, and prestige over the past three decades, women are less happy today than their predecessors were in 1972, both in absolute terms and relative to men.

Somewhere along the line we have bought into an external version of what "having and being it all" means. We are attracted to the approval of others, so we rise to each and every occasion, pushing ourselves beyond reasonable limits, without adequate regeneration and rejuvenation, only to perpetuate this self-defeating trap. We can't waste our education and skills just staying at home and yet we are still responsible for keeping the household in order and meeting the emotional and physical needs of the family, all while being pushed to move faster, harder, and higher up the ladder. If we added all the things that we do, expect ourselves to do, or feel that we should do in all of our roles, there is no way it would equate to one human being living in a single lifetime. We would have to be superhuman with superpowers, yet that is exactly what we set out to do every morning.

We may be armed with a degree and work accomplishments, but we will forever be frustrated if we don't differentiate between our expectations based on external factors and what we want in life based on what is important to us personally. A great conversation to have with our girlfriends is to discuss how much pressure we are putting on ourselves versus how much we feel pressured by external factors. For example, has our desire to be beautiful gone from empowerment to never-ending pressure? No doubt, our society judges and values beauty based on the outside more than the inside. When most people look at women, they often look for elements of beauty first. Even research has shown that women have a better chance at success in love and career if they simply look good[20]. Furthermore, the mass media is feeding into this by establishing narrow and unrealistic standards of beauty[21].

HAVING YOUR ALL

Most women want to look good and consequentially feel good about them selves, yet is it possible to have big breasts, a skinny waist, no cellulite, and Michelle Obama arms all at once? In modern society, it feels like women are showing more concern for beauty than for their own health[22]. There is an extreme strain for women to diet and match the images they see on the billboards and on television. It's an ideal that is seemingly unachievable by most women without psychological and physical consequences. Being "skinny" may just be the biggest pressure women feel today!

The modern woman is trying to do it all and it's not working[18]. Remember the question we asked earlier: Is it your innate and deep down belief that being "everything to everybody" is both desirable and possible? Unfortunately, our busy, over-committed lifestyles always come with consequences, and one of the biggest ones is that we are turning into "exhausted women" trying to make our expectations turn into a reality.

Meet Jenna, a 43-year-old single, female client who works in the technology industry on the West Coast.

<u>Jenna's day as planned in her mind:</u>
Rise and shine to NPR and the top of the hour news update at 6:00 am. Wake up feeling refreshed after a good night's sleep. Set an intention for what to accomplish today and then hit the treadmill for a quick 30-minute run followed by crunches and some toning exercises before getting ready for work. Have my outfit prepped from the night before and sit down to eat my favorite breakfast of blueberries, sliced almonds, and Greek yogurt so I can head into work feeling energized and ready for the day! Feel productive throughout the day and accomplish everything according to my time management system. Head out with colleagues for lunch at the healthy Thai restaurant, a fifteen minute walk away. It feels good to get a short walk out in the sunshine, eat tasty food, and laugh with colleagues. The rest of the day goes by quickly as it always does with interesting work. Leave work feeling empowered. Change into biking gear once at home to meet up with some friends. We have an upcoming trip to France to bike the Tour de France course. It's always been a dream and it's exhilarating trying to make it a reality. Finish the long ride with dinner with the biking group. Come home, shower, grab a glass of wine, and end the day with some

phone calls to friends and family followed by reading my next book club book before going to sleep. Love the feel of clean sheets and a productive day!

<u>*Jenna's day as it actually happens:*</u>
The alarm goes off at 6:00 am. I hit snooze three times and ignore the news. I did not get a good night's sleep after staying up late last night. Blurry-eyed and groggy, I stare at my closet trying to figure out what to wear. No time for a workout or breakfast now. Get ready and rush straight to work with a large cup of coffee in hand. Feel rushed and two steps behind all day. Need to make sure I have my reports ready earlier so there isn't this last-minute craziness. By 10:30, my stomach is screaming at me and I'm starting to scream orders to my assistant. Grab a handful of candy from the jar on her desk and grab my fourth cup of coffee. Need to get through this last meeting! It's lunchtime finally! I head down to the cafeteria in our building. The pizza line is the shortest again, so two slices, a Caesar salad, and large Diet Coke. Head back to my desk to eat so I can catch up on e-mails. The day goes on and I'm feeling like the cat dragged me in. There is too much to do and I'm so tired. Everything is taking longer than it needs to and I'm not even ready for a presentation tomorrow. End up skipping the bike ride I was going to take after work so I can work at home. I was hoping to plan a biking trip in France next season, but there just isn't enough time right now. Grab dinner from the take-out place on the way home and settle down to eat and work at my kitchen table with a glass of wine. One glass turns to three glasses by the time I finish the work. It's late, but finally a chance for some 'me' time. Craving a little treat after a long day, I grab a bag of chips to help settle the alcohol and sit down to watch something mindless. The day is finally done, but oops—it looks like I'm heading toward another late night!

Obviously Jenna wasn't able to match her intentions with her reality. The playbook in Jenna's head describes how she wants her day to go, but in the real game of life her day unfolds quite differently. Like most of us, she expects herself to "have it all"—the perfect balance of work and play, the stimulating activities, engaging support system, and healthy habits. What she ends up with is disappointment and frustration because day after day, her expectations are not in line with the choices she is making in her life. What Jenna does end up being is tapped out, burned out, and exhausted!

Although women have been running ragged for decades, spreading themselves thin trying to put enough of their time and energy into all their responsibilities, a new and more worrisome psychological shift is starting to occur. Women are beginning to accept exhaustion as a normal state of being. "Women can get so used to feeling lousy that they don't remember what it's like to feel good," says sleep medicine specialist Katherine Sharkey, M.D., Ph.D. With serious fatigue comes a continuous rush of the stress hormone cortisol, which can act as a mental and physical stimulant. Because of this, says Debbie Mandel, author of *Addicted to Stress*[23], "Highly charged women often don't sense that they're burning out. They get addicted to the high of accomplishment." What they don't realize, however, is just how impaired they are by their exhaustion, which can lead to a whole shopping list of physical and psychological woes. Ask yourself:

- Is being and doing everything for everyone part of my version of success?
- Is this really what I want?
- How successful have I been in achieving it?
- Could it be time to throw out the gender roles, throw out what others around me are doing, and throw out my own preconceived notions of what a successful woman's life should be?
- Am I exhausted from carrying around my over-loaded and unhealthy "full-plate"?

PART II

Struggling with the Juggling

CHAPTER FOUR

Should We Lean In, Lean Out or Just Stay in Bed?

Unfortunately, being exhausted is now just merely part of the world we live in. We've been taught to prize fatigue as a mark of achievement, as if a busy life equates to a successful life. If we're not exhausted, we're not doing enough[24]. This is exactly where so many of our clients feel their sense of exhaustion from—the pressure to constantly improve ourselves and the ambition to get more done so we can control and manage all of the various tasks and responsibilities in our lives. We keep telling ourselves that life will be better once we get that promotion, have enough money saved, get our kids into college, or lose those last ten pounds!

Experts also point to a need for validation that often drives women to never say "no" and keep piling on commitments to their plates. There is an undercurrent of pride in feeling important and in demand that "being busy" elicits. It seems we are starting to make this a part of our identity because it either serves a purpose or we truly need to improve on our time and life management skills. Perhaps "being busy" is a distraction from acknowledging certain realities in our lives that we now have an excuse not to deal with. Oops, too much going on to deal with the heavy "stuff." Anyone remember our mothers complaining to their friends about how busy they were or how stressed they were feeling when we were growing up?

Even women who switch their focus from the career track to the mommy track don't necessarily slow down; they just shift lanes from overachieving and long work hours in the workplace to the "doing it all" and "doing it perfectly" version of mommy-hood. In today's world, women aren't just keeping up with the Jones'; they're also keeping up with the Kardashians and all the other forms of distorted reality we are being fed by the media.

So we go through life like a kid in the candy store, saying "yes" to this, that, and everything we come across because we finally can. We say "yes" to work travel. "Yes" to having children in our forties. "Yes" to taking board positions on our favorite charities. "Yes" to so much all at once that somewhere along the way, we forgot how to say "no." We became "people-pleasers" and "good girls" that fulfill the roles and expectations for being perfect workers, mothers, and homemakers. We forgot that there are only 24 hours in each day and now we have said "yes" so many times that instead of leading our lives, our lives are leading us.

In 2012, there were many conversations debating if women can truly "have it all." *The Atlantic* had a cover piece debating the topic[1]. Working Women Media, talk shows, women's events, the blogosphere, celebrities, and columnists all weighed in with their opinions. The general consensus was either, "no, you can't have it all" or "yes, you can but not all at the same time." What has made "having it all" such a hot topic is the gradual withering of the "Superwoman" myth that was so highly prized in the 80s and 90s when women were determined to achieve equal success as men in the workplace and the glass ceilings were breaking. Women were finally able to achieve success in the same arenas that were closed off to their mother's generation, and they were storming in wearing their power suits and tennis shoes. We could all, even minorities, be Claire Huxtable of *The Cosby Show*, with the supportive marriage, respectful career, financial security, and the wonderful family. The media gave us example after example of "Superwomen" who were having it all and we took it all in.

What's changed since then? Well, first of all, we have figured out that what you see on TV and in magazines is not sustainable in reality. Life has also become even more complicated and fast-paced and technology has given us the ability to do, see, read, and go after even more. Work and personal lives have blended to create the opportunity to work at any given moment. Traditional roles are disintegrating with no clear distinction of who should take on breadwinner, household, and childcare duties. We encourage our daughters to be both soccer players and cheerleaders. Some of the most successful chefs and interior designers are male. There is an organic, underlying confusion as to who and what men and women should be and what life should look like. Not such a bad thing if we are comfortable defining what is most important and meaningful to us, but still a challenge if we are influenced by the whims of societal expectations and the media.

Meet Maya, a client that shared the chaos she went through in order to take a Christmas card picture that portrays how wonderful her life is and how well she is doing to her friends and family. The picture turned out beautifully with her three kids, husband, and dog sitting on rocks overlooking the sparkling Pacific Ocean. No one, however, knew the preparation it took Maya to get everyone matching white shirts with khaki bottoms and for her twin boys to be able to keep their clothes clean in time for the picture. The dog had to be groomed, she had to make hair and nail appointments for herself, and she changed the photographer appointment three times in order to get the perfect weather day. In the end, it took bribery with the kids, yelling at the dog, and frantic urgency to catch the sunset before she was able to get that perfect image!

It's a great example of the craziness many women go through to show perfection on the outside instead of working on what's important on the inside. We often feel the need to make our lives show like a glossy magazine, and both traditional and social media are not letting up in pointing out all the things women should be. It's so easy to feel inadequate and sometimes even envious when we see pictures of our friends' exotic vacations and read their seemingly forever happy posts on social media platforms. There's danger, however, in just seeing the carefully chosen highlights of people's lives when compared to the messy and chaotic reality that sometimes depicts our own lives. In a survey conducted by the TODAY show of 7,000 U.S. mothers, 75% report that the pressure they put on themselves is worse than any pressure or judgment they get from other moms. The same survey pointed out that 42% of these women suffer from "Pinterest Stress"—the worry that they're not crafty or creative enough. As blogger, Glennon Doyle Melton pointed out, "Stop the Pinsanity ... I don't know of any study that ever said kids turn out better if they have rainbow colored birthday cakes. Why are we doing this to ourselves?"[25].

In our work with women, we call the expectation to succeed in the workplace and yet be a fabulous homemaker, hostess, spouse, and mother "being Martha"—as in Martha Stewart, the seemingly perfect chef, crafter, decorator, gardener, and incredibly successful business woman of a multi-million dollar empire. We forget that she has a whole staff behind her helping to brand this image and that she is not that "perfect" given some of the choices she has made in her life. Yet, wouldn't it be great to catch her eating her breakfast in the car like the rest of us, rather than as her image appears to portray at a perfectly set breakfast table with organic homemade food items and fresh flowers?

Let's also be very clear that "having it all" doesn't just refer to balancing work life with family and home life. After all, women with families who have to work out of necessity may not even have the luxury to engage in this debate; they have to do both for the sake of survival. Many of these women, especially single mothers, are not worrying about "having it all," but rather about having enough to just get through the day! On the flip-side, women who don't have to and choose not to have a paying job still struggle with life-balance from everything they seem to fill their plates with. They take on large commitments within the community or schools to compensate for not working outside of the home.

And what about those women who don't have a family yet or are choosing not to? As blogger Clementine Ford from the Daily Life wrote, "I'm not even really sure what "having it all" is supposed to look like. Is it being enabled to have a meaningful, satisfying career and a family to go home to at the end of the day? For a supposedly feminist preoccupation, it ignores the diverse interests and realities of large proportions of women and those for whom children and/or career were either undesirable or impossible. According to this definition, as a child-free, unmarried woman in her early 30s, I would appear to fall rather short of having much of anything at all." We all exist within our own trying to "have it all" paradigm[26].

This past year, another external expectation came our way as we were encouraged to "lean in" and strive to achieve our highest potential within the workplace and in life. According to Sheryl Sandberg's bestseller, *Lean In*[27], "We hold ourselves back in ways both big and small, by lacking self-confidence, by not raising our hands, and by pulling back when we should be leaning in." We are encouraged to take our seat at the table, change how we speak to command more authority, and even resist slowing down in order to seek more equality.

Are we really blaming women for not trying hard enough, and are we continuing to hold women to unattainable standards of personal and professional success as challenged by professor and author, Anne-Marie Slaughter? Many of the women we interviewed for this book expressed their frustration at having to add on even more to their mental to-do lists. They now have to "show-up" even more at work in order to succeed in the workplace and represent the female gender in the boardroom and the government. It's leaving women with the feeling that they are never doing enough and that they always need to work harder and even one-up those around them in order to be successful in their lives. As one executive described, "If I lean in anymore, I'm going to fall over!"

Although we respect and admire the overall vision of what Sheryl Sandberg is attempting, the push for women to work harder for equality doesn't seem to be the best approach for supporting the needs of most women. Most of us do not have the stock riches, support staff, and helpful partner that Sandberg has. Most working women in our country are struggling with cash flow and childcare and are often single or in unsupportive marriages. We need solutions that are personalized to our lives and needs, and solutions that speak to our individual stages of life. We also need better support and more flexibility in the workplace for both men and women to balance their personal responsibilities and job duties. What we don't need are the expectations to be like "Martha" at home and "Sheryl" at work!

CHAPTER FIVE
Stress: 9-5 and Beyond

Stress is partly a social disease—an adaptation to social and cultural conditions. No doubt, the lives of American women have improved in many ways, but measures of subjective well-being indicate that women's happiness has declined during the past 35 years[28]. The problem is, while taking on new opportunities, women are still maintaining the majority of the traditional roles, including the responsibilities for child-rearing and home maintenance. Add to the mix the stress of maintaining physical attractiveness and being exposed to the same stressors that men typically experience in their roles as high-achieving and driven workers. All of it is enough to make a woman's life feel like a pressure cooker!

As a result, high achieving women are paying the physical and psychological price to obtain equal opportunity[29]. Society has yet to iron out all of the details on how to spread out these responsibilities with better balance. Having to face constant change and not having control over their boundaries are some of the top stressors and challenges women leaders face, according to the Creative Leadership Institute[30]. As a response to society and their own expectations, women have learned to simply accept exhaustion as a normal state of being in today's world[31].

HAVING YOUR ALL

Meet Donna, one of our clients who described herself as a "cranky, tired woman who is not so fun to be around" when she first began to work with us:

Donna is trying to do it all in Dallas. She is a 49-year-old single mother of two teenagers and owner and manager of a group of franchised hair salons that are monetarily successful, but require constant oversight in order to run smoothly. Her kitchen is being renovated, which means she's living in a construction zone; her boys are star athletes requiring extra transportation, snacks, and loads of laundry; and they have a new puppy that is not quite getting the concept of potty-training. Add to that the constant staff hires, paperwork, and management responsibilities she has to maintain for her business and you can see that Donna is exhausted! Overwhelmed and anxious, she is having trouble sleeping and has no desire to take care of herself even if she had the time and energy to do so. She has lost interest in just about everything, her body aches all over, and she's suffering from stomach cramps and irregular bowels. She's tired of juggling it all and just wants to crawl into bed and pull the covers over her head!

Is there hope for Donna? How do you feel right now…zippy or zapped? Stress comes to us in two different packages. It can be brought on acutely by sudden, negative changes in circumstances like a tragic car accident or the death of a loved one. Or it can be the routine chronic stress like what Donna is experiencing that is related to work pressures, family life, and other responsibilities. Chronic stress is long-term, unrelenting, feels inescapable, and wears your body, mind, and spirit down. It creates tension, restlessness, irritability, and it results in overwhelm and exhaustion. It is this type of stress that can lead to serious physical and mental health consequences if not managed properly.

Adrenaline is the main hormone triggered in acute stress and cortisol is the main hormone released in chronic stress. We need both in order to survive threats to our safety, as seen in the "fight or flight" response; however, the stress reaction was never intended to be turned on too high, too often, or for too long. Most causes of stress today cannot be overcome by fighting or fleeing, but rather must be endured on a daily basis as in Donna's case. The never-ending deadlines, intimidating boss, financial worries, and external pressures to do all and be all to everyone is enough to keep cortisol flowing through our bodies and wreak havoc on our health and well-being.

An enormous number of studies have now shown us that stress negatively impacts nearly every single body system, from the gut to the heart, from the brain to the bones, and from the muscles to the mind. Stress has an effect on our cardiovascular, digestive, immune, and psychological systems, along with our brain functioning. Anywhere from 60 to 90% of physician visits have been attributed to stress-related concerns[32]. There is also evidence that stress accelerates aging, and we all know that it seems to steal the joy from our lives. Most important, feeling stressed and overwhelmed prevents us from doing all that we desire and from being the best that we can be in all the different areas of our lives.

Stress shows up in women's bodies in many different ways. Understanding if your body is being affected by stress is the first step to making changes in your life. Check off the following stress side effects to see if you feel zippy for the most part or zapped and ready to crawl into bed like Donna.

Physical symptoms:
- [ ] Headaches
- [ ] Insomnia
- [ ] Fatigue
- [ ] Appetite changes
- [ ] Dependency on smoking
- [ ] High consumption of alcohol
- [ ] Drug use

Emotional:
- [ ] Anxiety
- [ ] Inability to control anger
- [ ] Unhappiness
- [ ] Irritability
- [ ] Depression
- [ ] Frustration

Mental:
- [ ] Forgetfulness
- [ ] Worry
- [ ] Inability to make decisions
- [ ] Negative thinking
- [ ] Boredom

Occupational:
- [ ] Work overwhelm
- [ ] Long hours to accomplish job
- [ ] Relationship conflicts
- [ ] Feeling unfulfilled with work

Social:
- [ ] Loneliness
- [ ] Family problems
- [ ] Inability to be intimate with others
- [ ] Isolation
- [ ] Resentment

Spiritual:
- [ ] Apathy
- [ ] Loss of meaning
- [ ] Emptiness
- [ ] Doubt
- [ ] Despair
- [ ] Guilt

If you are experiencing more than half of these symptoms right now, then your health and well being are potentially jeopardized and need to become more of a priority. Your body is not meant to be walking around all day in this state, and you know that it's not very enjoyable or productive.

It's a given that we tend to experience stress because of the people and places where we spend most of our time. As we are working more hours and as technology enables work to seep into our recreational time, work stressors tend to rise to the top of our personal well-being challenges. When the stress response is turned on for too long, it drains the body of energy and leads to fatigue, exhaustion, and burnout. This release of cortisol for extended periods of time slows down brain processing and affects emotional and physical health[33].

Take a look at the impact of stress to personal performance and imagine the effects to overall workplace productivity:

- Decreased mental function
- Short-term memory loss
- Difficulty with focus on tasks
- Scattered and fragmented thinking
- Avoidance of decision-making
- Decreased creativity
- Diminished work output
- Decreased efficiency
- Physical fatigue
- Mentally exhausted
- Emotionally overwhelmed
- Greater workplace dissatisfaction
- Lower energy levels
- Poor and costly decision making
- More time wasted
- Difficult and negative attitudes

- Moodiness
- Increased worry and anxiety
- Decreased cooperation
- Impatience and short tempers
- Depression
- Greater employee absenteeism
- Higher worker turnover
- Difficulty processing new information
- Easily distracted

Basically, if you're feeling overwhelmed and exhausted, you're not able to do your best work. The World Health Organization calls stress the health epidemic of the 21st century, and the cost to American employers is estimated at $300 billion per year[34]. That's a hefty price for companies to pay as stress hits them below the belt with lower productivity, absenteeism, staff turnover, workers' compensation, medical insurance, and related expenses. Most employers would agree that employee stress is directly linked to profits and that it is the number one factor related to productivity.

In our many years of working with busy executives and our front-row seats within the work culture of many corporations, this is the way we see the problem:

1. The pace of life is too fast, responsibilities are too many, expectations are high both internally and externally, the pressure to perform to perfection is too great, and support systems are too few.

2. The combination of all these factors leads to high levels of stress, strong feelings of overwhelm, the need to be working all the time, and personal self-neglect.

3. Temporary strategies and poor coping skills are used for quick fixes to stress, such as overeating junk food, drinking too much

alcohol, doing drugs as an escape, amping up on large amounts of caffeine for energy bursts, or engaging in destructive distractions.

4. These quick fixes turn into lifestyle habits that lead to chronic stress, fatigue, weight gain, depression, and eventually move on to more serious physical and mental illnesses.

5. We are functioning in this "dis-eased" state, with low energy levels and negative feelings, which turns many of us into moody, impatient, and short tempered beings in the workplace and at home.

6. We have more conflict and decreased morale in the workplace and more strain and interpersonal stress in our relationships at home.

7. We end up decreasing our performance and productivity both in our work and our personal lives and we don't feel good mentally or physically[31].

Women also feel different stressors at work based on what motivates them. According to research from the The Center for Talent and Innovation, men are highly motivated by money and power and women by wanting to have factors related to more balance in their life. The following reasons highlight the top seven motivations women have when looking for a job[35]:

<u>Working Woman's Wish List</u>
1. Time for family
2. Meaning and purpose in work
3. Valuable colleagues
4. Giving back to society in their work
5. Healing the planet
6. Want of flexibility
7. Money and power

If these seven factors are not integrated into our work or are not part of the structure of the workplace, there will be a great sense of inner stress for most women. Examine your own work life and see if there are any connections to the Working Woman's Wish List above as to your unmanaged sources of chronic stress.

How about stressors at home? Of all the places you expect to feel free from stress, home can instead be a potential minefield of stress triggers. Take a look…

Meet Lenae, a 37-year-old human resources manager who has tried in vain to get her two young children to eat their chicken nuggets. She tried coaxing, pleading, and then finally bribing with jello for dessert. The kids just fidgeted, whined, and fought with each other. It was the last thing Lenae needed after a hectic and long workday, 35 minutes of battling traffic, and coming home to a house full of clutter, scattered toys, and piles of laundry with her name on it, not to mention the unfinished work e-mails she needed to tackle by the morning. Lenae asked her husband to take the boys up for their baths while she cleared up the kitchen. When he didn't respond after the second time, she raised her voice and snapped that she "can't do it all and would love a little help once in awhile!" Her heart rate shot up, she could feel the acid building in her stomach, and she felt deflated. She was turning into ticking time bomb that could explode at any minute—she just couldn't seem to get a handle on her life!

Women experience excessive pressure and overwhelming responsibilities at home just as much as they do at work[36]. This is especially true for working moms, like Lenae, who juggle the demands and expectations of the workplace for most of the day, only to come home to face the needs of children, spouses, pets, and the constant upkeep of maintaining a home.

Work can feel like an escape in comparison! One of our executive female clients even said that the most stressful time of her day is getting her kids off to school before she heads to work. By the time the bus comes to pick them up in the morning, she starts her day with her heart rate up and her breakfast churning in her stomach.

HAVING YOUR ALL

Managing all of our human relationships and responsibilities presents a daily challenge. Everyone wants and needs things and women seem to be at the center, trying to fulfill all those obligations. For example, Lenae's long work hours, high level job responsibility, and her need to bring her work home have a negative effect on her home life. She experiences a significant sense of overwhelm and the feeling of having too much on her plate. In the same way, Lenae's home life, her fragile partnership with her husband, financial worries, and childcare concerns negatively affect her ability to focus and do her job as effectively.

What becomes a vicious cycle with the conflicting demands of work and home causes excessive stress and eventually poor health. Lenae loses out, as does her family, her employer, and our society as a whole. And it's not only physical stressors related to too many responsibilities and not enough time—it's the psychological factors as well.

Take a look at some of the internal and mental stressors we find women face:

- *Feeling overwhelmed.* This feeling of having too much on our plates comes up over and over again. There are too many tasks to do, too little time to do them, too many things to think about, too many places to be, and too many people wanting things from us! We have overflowing plates!

- *Lack of recognition for all we do.* Women are still not getting enough R-E-S-P-E-C-T. We are still underpaid in the workplace and feel unappreciated at home[36]. We want to be periodically acknowledged and thanked for all that we do for others.

- *The pressure to keep up.* Not only do we have to work hard, keep a home, and raise a family, but we also have to look good doing it[37]! The expectations to do so many things and to do them perfectly are overwhelming.

- *Having to multi-task all the time.* The pace of life is just too fast for only doing one task at a time. There are too many unrealistic

- *Drama.* Whether it's tensions with family or work, the potential for interpersonal conflict can make our environments so much more stressful.

- *Technology.* What should be making our lives easier is instead adding information overload and the pressure to constantly socially network. E-mails, texts, blogs, Facebook, Pinterest, Instagram , tweets … the list goes on and will continue to grow as the latest technology ends up adding one more thing to our perpetual to-do list.

- *Guilt.* The big, bad, ugly word in women's lives. When we are at work, we are worrying about letting the ball drop at home and when at home, we worry about not doing enough for our work. With longer hours, higher expectations, advanced technology, and a down turn economy, the lines are now blurred as there is no separation of work and home life. As such, we feel pressured to be doing both at all times[38].

The bottom line is that women are overwhelmed and exhausted! If someone asks you, "How are things going?" what would you answer? Life is crazy, insane, and super-busy? Does anyone ever answer with something positive anymore? We race from one activity or responsibility to another, stretching ourselves to the limit and rarely taking the time to relax. We feel pressured, rushed, edgy, and…stressed! It's time to make a change.

CHAPTER SIX

The "Evolved" Woman

So now we know that **frenzied lives and overflowing plates are making us stressed.** It doesn't feel good mentally and physically, and we know it's taking a toll on our immediate productivity and our long-term health. "The way we define success isn't working. More, bigger, better—we can't do that anymore," Arianna Huffington, the editor-in-chief of the Huffington Post Media Group, was quoted as saying in the New York Times. "If we don't redefine success, the personal price we pay will get higher and higher. And as the data shows, that price is even higher for women than for men. Already women in stressful jobs have a nearly 40% increased risk of heart disease and a 60% greater risk for diabetes," she says in her 2013 commencement speech to Smith college. "The answer? To create a movement that embraces the idea that physical and spiritual wellness—from meditation to exercise to good nutrition—are integral to, not separate from, a successful life," she concludes in the article[39].

We don't want to be exhausted women! We prefer to be "evolved" women who have figured out how to balance our well-being with our responsibilities and move ourselves forward toward our own version of success. Or how about …

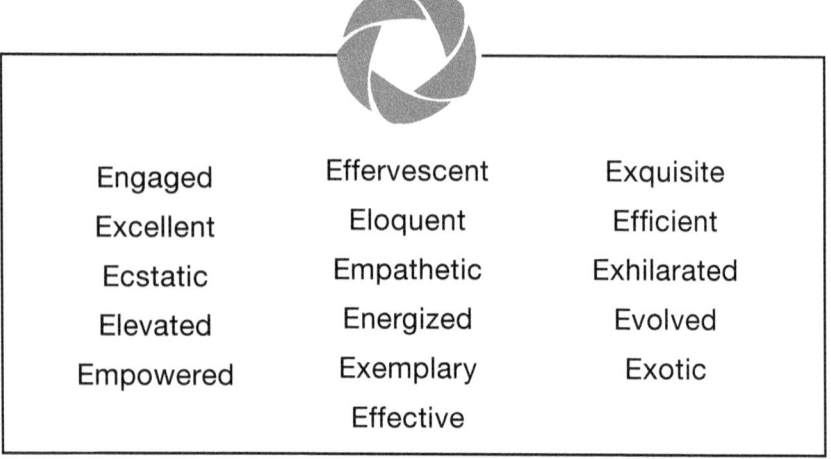

Engaged	Effervescent	Exquisite
Excellent	Eloquent	Efficient
Ecstatic	Empathetic	Exhilarated
Elevated	Energized	Evolved
Empowered	Exemplary	Exotic
	Effective	

Choose what kind of "e-woman" you would rather be. Which of these words, or any others, describes the attitude and characteristics you want to exude?

Transformation toward well-being and success is all about evolution. We have chosen three words that depict what we find women really value and want more of in their lives: ENERGY, EMPOWERMENT, and being EFFECTIVE. These three qualities can help move you away from a life filled with expectations and stressors and more toward living a life that is healthy and balanced. You have the *energy* to accomplish what is good for your body and mind, you feel *empowered* to go after what is meaningful to you in life, and you lead an *effective* life that enables you to accomplish goals and achieve your success. Basically, you have the tools to having "your" all.

ENERGIZED – To have staying power to do your best and work hard without losing focus or steam, both at home and at work. Energy gives you a boost and makes your days productive and fulfilled. Feeling super-charged makes life more exciting and you are able to tackle your responsibilities with more enthusiasm. Lack of energy, on the other hand—from physical, psychological or emotional drain—is a top concern physicians hear from women today. Physical and mental energy can be the result of exercise, stress reduction, being in balance, rejuvenation and rest, and from feeling connected to others. Energized women radiate and sparkle!

EMPOWERED – To take advantage of opportunities, control your destiny, and be proactive in seeking what you want in life. Empowered means feeling strong and having the attitude that "nothing can stop me" and that "I can handle whatever comes my way." Empowered women are confident, know what they want, and give themselves permission to align their well-being with their values, passions, and sense of purpose. You feel empowered when you can move onto what really matters to you and increase your spiritual, political, social, educational, gender, and economic strengths, both as individuals and as role models in your community.

EFFECTIVE – To have the ability to plan ahead and make choices suited for you so that your journey runs smoothly, supporting the results you want to see. When you're effective, you are creative, curious, and self-motivated. You are prepared without needing to be over prepared. Effective symbolizes productive and results-oriented women. They have focus and clear mindsets. Effective women get things done! They are rested, manage their stress, and they feel that they are in control of their lives.

So, are you ready to evolve toward a new way of living, thinking, prioritizing, and balancing? Being more energized, empowered, and effective is what you can look forward to when you put self-care in a prime spot on your plate. In our Power Habits section of the book, the strategies and suggestions we present will provide specific actions you can take to move toward living with these three qualities strongly established in your life.

In the meantime, you can see how different life can look when you shift your mindset toward a life of balance and well-being as priorities, while making decisions that leave "exhaustion" off your plate. Meet Sandra, a newly married 33-year-old Product Manager for a large technology company in Seattle. She is an example of the next generation of women who understand that they have choices and are being more thoughtful about what they want in their lives and mindful to include self-care into the equation[40].

HAVING YOUR ALL

Sandra says her workplace success has moved her forward on the path to become a director in the near future, but that she is not interested in doing what it takes to become a vice president just yet. Sandra and her husband met while working for the company after getting their MBAs when they were both young superstars within their own divisions. Although she worked long hours, Sandra made it a priority to have a girl's night out once a week, grab a run every day, and take a couple's yoga class every Sunday morning followed by brunch. They both cherished their work and put long hours in, but she said that they both knew they didn't want to work at this pace for the long haul. As they began to plan their future together, other priorities became important to them, like spending time with their extended families. They now had nieces and nephews that they wanted to create memories with. They enjoy work nights and weekends going to concerts and dinners out with other couples compared to working long days and on the weekends.

Their five-year vision, which they have thoroughly discussed, involves a family and not a VP-level title for either of them at this time. They expect each other to contribute to the childrearing and that both of them will need to make sacrifices to their careers ... and they are okay with that. They want to enjoy their time together and their years as parents, and they have no desire to put all their eggs in one basket. They feel confident that both of their incomes will provide for a comfortable life that enables them to enjoy all of their interests. They seek experiences more than owning possessions and really value their well-being[41]. Sandra said their fear was that if they kept pushing forward on their career tract, they would have more money to spend, but no time to actually spend it! They are clear on their priorities, which makes it easier to say "no" to the things that aren't meaningful to them. What they are saying "yes" to instead is a three-month sabbatical/delayed honeymoon to travel the world backpacking ... without their computers in tow!

Sandra is part of the next generation of women who are challenging female roles, whether traditional or modern, to "evolve" toward creating a life that works for them as an individual. Sandra, like many other millennial women her age that reached adulthood around the year 2000, has worked incredibly hard throughout all of her schooling to position herself for executive and high-income careers. She, however, wants to avoid the pitfalls and burnout that has many women leaving the workplace prematurely [41].

According to research conducted by McKinsey, 53% of corporate entry-level jobs are held by women today, which drops to 37% for mid-management roles and 26% for vice presidents and senior managers[42]. The high rate of drop-out for female executives mid-career is a major challenge in getting more women to reach the top positions within business and politics. It's tough to keep going hard at the same pace while still maintaining so many of the traditionally female roles and responsibilities.

Data from the PR firm Zeno Group indicates that only 15% of women between the ages of 21 and 33 have the desire to lead a large or prominent organization[43]. It seems that women, like Sandra just aren't willing to make the personal sacrifices and compromises they perceive female leaders have to make in order to be successful. Ninety percent of these women surveyed also believe that female executives are forced to make greater sacrifices than male executives. They are aware of the institutional barriers and the additional stressors female leaders still face and are choosing to opt out of the process or at least modify their own pathway to the top.

Although they are experiencing stressors from the shifting job outlook and the economic ups and downs, the women of this generation that we interviewed have the confidence to know what fulfils them and they greatly value their well-being. As a result, they are shedding traditional female roles and expectations and are showing us that life balance is an issue that both genders, the workplace, and society must address.

This next generation also values fun, enjoys freedom of choice, and desires to control and balance their work and home life[39]. *The Washington Post* and Pew Research Center conducted a poll that indicated millennial women are better-educated, ambitious, optimistic, and determined to enjoy a more well-rounded life than their mothers' overstressed generation. This doesn't mean we won't see any female CEOs of large companies or a female president in the upcoming years; rather, it's important to acknowledge that a generational shift is occurring. These women are not willing to sacrifice what they value and their own personal happiness in order to excel solely in their work life. It's just not enough for them anymore.

So, what can we all learn from these "evolved" younger women and the choices they are making? We sum it up with the visual of a stairwell with landings on each floor. There is an opportunity to pause at each landing to catch your breath and evaluate before heading up again versus rushing up the traditional ladder that heads straight up with no breaks at all. Each pause enables you to redefine your goals according to your current reality and come up with newly-laid-out measures of success in order to thrive in all the parts of your life, including your well-being.

The future is brighter as this new generation moves forward into an unchartered landscape. Millennial women are not only starting to redefine what "having it all" means, but they are also practicing it. They are prime examples of our future "e-women"—shifting from exhausted to extraordinary!

PART III

Having "Your" All

CHAPTER SEVEN
Define Your Success

What really matters to us most is what we value. A life well-lived is one that is filled with the things that we personally find the most meaningful. Our value systems are internal to us and are directly tied to our individual success. They influence our beliefs and consequently affect our behavior. Knowing and understanding what we value is so important because it guides our decisions and defines our lives. Once we understand what we value, we are better able to pick and choose our priorities to be able to determine what and how much to put on to our plates.

Author Patricia H. Sprinkle offers wise words in her book *Women Who Do Too Much*[44]: "Our goal should not be to become hyper-organized, highly efficient Superwomen; our goal should be to spend most of our time on what we value most." So much of the unhappiness and frustration women experience is based on living lives that they are not even sure they want.

> Being more organized and efficient with tasks and commitments we don't value will never lead to the long-term and meaningful success we are striving for.

When our values align with our work and play, life feels more joyful and balanced. Our work becomes more fulfilling and tends to be more effective as a result. When they are not aligned, something seems out of sorts. We are easily discontented, unmotivated, and disengaged with our work and our lives. This tends to lead to higher rates of burnout at work and harmful personal behaviors. On the other hand, a common quality in effective leaders is that they are crystal clear about what is important to them and exhibit their values in all of their actions and in their leadership style. They are able to influence others because most people can sense when someone is living a genuine and authentic life—their values are aligned with their actions and life. They are not emulating someone else's way of life; instead, they are successful because they are being themselves.

The definition of success means different things to different people, mainly because each of us holds differing values within us and within our separate experiences and exposures. There are no right and wrong values, but you want to be able to differentiate between your personal values and those outside of you that have the greatest influence in your life. Society may have us interpreting success as the American Dream, with its external signs of success of more money, fancy cars, big homes, or prestigious job titles. We see this often with our clients who seem to "have it all" according to these markers, but who experience deep-seated unhappiness and dissatisfaction in their lives. They end up turning to quick fixes like shopping or overindulging in food or alcohol to "fill them up" with good feelings that are short-lived and destructive to their overall health and well-being. They may come in wanting to lose weight, but they end up needing to revaluate the bigger picture of their lives before they can really make a permanent difference in their health.

We also hear about the success stories of both men and women who leave the "rat race" to find joy in running a B & B in the country. Somewhere along the way, they recognized that the life they were leading was not in line with what was important to them, and they made life decisions to place themselves in an environment that was more aligned with what they valued. They worked hard in the city and they are still working hard in a different capacity in the country, but there is more contentment in their lives now. It all ends up reflecting positively in their health and well-being. This is success defined by you—the person who actually has to live your life and is the essence of "having YOUR all"!

Meet Tonia, one of our inspirational clients that we also partner with in supporting women's organizations.

Tonia worked with us in her company-sponsored leadership program. She was at an uninspired stage of her career, feeling sluggish in her health, energy, and with her productivity at work. Instead of trying to put temporary fixes on her specific problems, we dug deep and discovered that Tonia's most important values were beginning to shift. She needed to connect her value of giving back and making a difference with a sense of purpose to her work. At one point in her life, she valued being financially secure, but she had now achieved this and needed to re-evaluate her values and reconnect her sense of passion and purpose to her work. Tonia took action and became re-energized by creating a mentoring program with support from her work. She not only empowered herself to live her values, but is also inspiring others to do so as well.

For Tonia, success means having made it out of the impoverished childhood she grew up in. Success was being the first in her family to go to college and graduate with honors. Success for Tonia is defined by being a manager at a large biomedical company and being able to provide for herself and her elderly mother. Success for Tonia also means spending her time and energy giving back to the community she came from and mentoring girls to stay committed to their education. Her life falls in line with what she values most: prosperity, achievement, and community. Tonia leads a successful life and is having her all!

So, what do you value the most? Have these values been a consistent part of your life? Do they need an update, as values do change over time as we mature and our circumstances in life change? Values, and therefore your focus, may change when you have new work, new family structures, and new relationships. What may have been the desire for status and money in earlier stages of your career can change to the hope of leaving a legacy or making a difference in the world later in your life. The key is to know what is important and meaningful to you at any given stage and let your values dictate your life actions and decisions.

What happens if your top three values include family, wealth, and ambition? Can all three of these work together at the same time? Working women sometimes have the greatest degree of conflict when it comes to living their values. The desire to bring home a consistent and hopefully large paycheck directly conflicts with the value of spending time with family and other personal relationships. That does not mean that family can't be part of a working mother's value system; rather, choices on how you spend your time and energy must now be strategic and well-planned. Working mothers need to be living their values both at work and at home. That type of consistency can help decide what goes on your plate and what needs to come off of it; what commitments you say "yes" to and which ones you graciously decline.

By this time you might be a little curious as to what values truly reflect what is meaningful to you. The following exercise will help you to discover your top ten values and then whittle them down to the three most influencing factors you want in your life right now. This exercise will help you differentiate what is important to you so that you can clear your plate of the things that you spend so much of your time and energy on, but that you are now recognizing may not be that valuable to you after all.

Step 1: What I Value Most...

From this list of values (both work and personal), select the ten that give you a spark of energy, feel exciting, and correlate with meaning in your life right now. Feel free to add any values of your own to this list.

- ☐ Accountability
- ☐ Achievement
- ☐ Adventurousness
- ☐ Affection
- ☐ Affluence
- ☐ Ambition
- ☐ Arts
- ☐ Balance
- ☐ Belonging
- ☐ Calmness
- ☐ Change
- ☐ Community
- ☐ Commitment
- ☐ Compassion
- ☐ Competence
- ☐ Competition
- ☐ Consistency
- ☐ Courtesy
- ☐ Creativity
- ☐ Curiosity
- ☐ Decisiveness
- ☐ Dependability
- ☐ Devoutness
- ☐ Discipline
- ☐ Diversity
- ☐ Excellence
- ☐ Expression/Style
- ☐ Expertise
- ☐ Exploration
- ☐ Elegance
- ☐ Empathy
- ☐ Enthusiasm
- ☐ Equality

☐ Fairness	☐ Justice	☐ Security
☐ Faith	☐ Knowledge	☐ Self-Control
☐ Family	☐ Leadership	☐ Selflessness
☐ Fame	☐ Loyalty	☐ Spirituality
☐ Financial gain	☐ Make a difference	☐ Serenity
☐ Friendship	☐ Money	☐ Service
☐ Fitness	☐ Nature	☐ Sophistication
☐ Focus	☐ Originality	☐ Simplicity
☐ Freedom	☐ Order	☐ Spontaneity
☐ Fun	☐ Perfectionism	☐ Stability
☐ Generosity	☐ Positivity	☐ Structure
☐ Goodness	☐ Practicality	☐ Success
☐ Growth	☐ Pleasure	☐ Status
☐ Greater Good	☐ Power	☐ Teaching
☐ Happiness	☐ Popularity	☐ Truth
☐ Hard Work	☐ Professionalism	☐ Teamwork
☐ Health	☐ Prestige	☐ Thankfulness
☐ Honesty	☐ Public Service	☐ Timeliness
☐ Humility	☐ Reliability	☐ Trustworthiness
☐ Hope	☐ Resourcefulness	☐ Unity
☐ Independence	☐ Recognition/Respect	☐ Vision
☐ Individuality	☐ Relationships	☐ Wealth
☐ Innovation	☐ Religion	☐ Well-being
☐ Integrity	☐ Reputation	☐ Wisdom
☐ Influencing others	☐ Resilience	☐ Work with others
☐ Joy	☐ Responsibility	☐ Working alone

Step 2: Elimination

Now that you have identified your top ten list, close your eyes and imagine yourself living your ideal life. What values are present in that vision? Which ones are not as prevalent in your imaginary life? Start crossing off some of the values that still may be important to you, but are not as integral to what you do in your day and how you lead your life. What three values did you choose to live your life based on?

MY TOP THREE VALUES

1. _____
2. _____
3. _____

From here, you want to go a step further and think about how to live your life with these three values at the forefront and through your habits, routines, and actions. Dig deeper and incorporate them into ways of being and living that not only lead to your version of success, but also to a deeper sense of well-being. Ask yourself:

- What am I yearning for?
- Where do I feel deprived in my life?
- What do I need more of right now?
- What do I need less of in my life?
- What are my absolute "no's" that I don't want to do anymore?

Be specific with your responses. Knowing "what you don't want to do" is just as important as knowing "what you do want to do." Be clear about what you refuse to tolerate in your life. Pay attention to the things that frustrate you. When do you typically feel tension, muscle tightening, or aches in your body?

By knowing and listening to your true reactions and not playing the roles you are used to playing, you can make life choices that honor your values and help you develop your own personal definition of success.

CHAPTER EIGHT

Living With Passion

"**Passion is energy. Feel the power that comes from focusing on what excites you.**" What a powerful quote from a powerful woman, Oprah Winfrey. You can almost feel the energy when you say the word "passion." It's the juice that makes you feel alive and keeps you moving. It's being happy from the inside out. Interestingly, it is passion, not money that seems to be one of the key drivers of success based on research by success expert, Richard St. John. Almost nothing great has been achieved without passion[45].

We love this definition of passion from Urban Dictionary: *"Passion is when you put more energy into something than is required to do it. It is more than just enthusiasm or excitement; passion is ambition that is materialized into action to put as much heart, mind, body and soul into something as is possible."*

Sorry, it's not the romantic version of passion we're asking you to focus on, although it's not a bad thing to have in your life! We are encouraging you to explore your passions in order for you to be able to achieve your personal and most meaningful success. The reason we're dedicating a whole chapter to it is that passion is such a powerful motivator. It turns "have-to's" into "want-to's." When passion is missing in our lives, our actions lack energy and we struggle to achieve the results we want. By the middle years of life when we're bogged down by numerous responsibilities and may have lost touch with our inner spark, passion can ignite us toward inspired action once again. Imagine spending the rest of your life working, supporting others, and never tapping into what truly brings you joy and fuels your soul. No, thank you!

Of course, success requires a lot more than just passion, and pursuing your passion while making a living is not always easy. Characteristics like hard work, courage, persistence, and commitment are also required components of getting the most out of life. Also, your passions may not coincide with your chosen work, so it requires finding time and opportunities in an already overscheduled lifestyle. However, most everyone would agree that it's worth the effort to live life with that extra "oomph" in it.

Meet Carol, one of our girlfriends living on the East Coast. She is a beautiful example of someone who had the courage to value her passion and choose to make it a priority in her life. Take a look…

Carol spent the first part of her career struggling between two choices: her parents wanting her to become a physician and Carol's innate love of piano and music. While in medical school, Carol continued to play and perform concerts on the side. While immersed in music, she found stress reduction, joy, and flow through the art of piano. Against her parent's wishes, Carol finally chose to follow what she valued: creativity, expression, and beauty in her work. That led her to her dream job as a concert pianist, master piano teacher, and now a sought after professional performer. Carol is living her life with passion and it's leading her to achieve success on her own terms.

Carol chose to give focus to what she was fueled by and not what her parents wanted her to do. If she continued with medicine, she would have sacrificed what she found most meaningful and she may have never experienced the energy and excitement that comes from engaging in something she truly loves. Instead, now she has a career enjoying piano and inspiring and teaching others to follow their dreams. Carol defined her own success based on the artistic expression that she both valued and was passionate about.

How can you get some of this passion into your life? Imagine waking up every morning knowing you're going to love and enjoy your day. Your life will be based on what intrinsically motivates you and not from external influencers and roles we tend to get stuck into. The following *Passion Pursuit* activity is an exercise to help you reconnect with your passions. This will increase your awareness of what should be part of your life plate and provide support to define your version of living a successful life.

Get ready to rediscover your passions by finding a quiet spot to reflect. Take a deep breath and start to look within as you answer the following questions. Forget the roles you live right now as a boss, mother, spouse, or house manager. Retreat into the past and tap into the dreams you had when you were younger or lived out when you were single. Reflect on what you naturally gravitated toward. It's time to get in touch with your true self and uncover what brings you the most joy and fulfillment. Answer the following questions:

- *When you were 8 years old how did you spend your free time?*
- *What were your three favorite subjects in high school?*
- *What sections in the bookstore do you naturally gravitate toward?*
- *What were your three greatest achievements in life thus far?*
- *What qualities are you most proud of in yourself?*
- *If all your necessities were taken care of, what would you do?*
- *What makes you come alive?*
- *What work feels like play no matter how many hours you put into it?*
- *Write down 10 goals that you want to accomplish. Then write next to them what is the thing you like most about that goal and how it relates to your values.*

HAVING YOUR ALL

What did you discover? Remember, you don't have to be good at something you're passionate about. It can simply be what you feel alive and joyful doing. Pursuing your passions in big ways or small can contribute to your overall levels of happiness and fulfillment. This might mean turning a passion of yours into your work, it may be a hobby you do on the side, or it may simply be the way you live your life. Uncovering your passion isn't a destiny, but rather a journey. You can have more than one passion, and your passions may change throughout your life. No matter how you live out your passions, let it contribute to your version of success and let it enhance your well-being, happiness, and quality of life. Watch out world—there are some passionate women running loose!

CHAPTER NINE

Choose Happy

Which comes first ... are successful women happier or does success make a woman happier? We're not sure we will ever be able to figure that one out completely, but both statements hold some truth to them. Technically, we should be the happiest generation of women in history. We don't need marriage for security and survival, and if we're miserable in our marriage we can easily divorce in today's world. We have legal contraception to determine if we want children and when. We have equal access to education and interesting and rewarding careers in all fields. We may even have partners who help out with household and domestic responsibilities.

> Compared to all the generations of women who came before us, we are seemingly living the dream that they never even thought imaginable!

Yet, we're not quite satisfied. Recent data has shown us that women are not as happy as they have been in the past regardless of financial status, marital position, children, age, and race[46]. As noted earlier, women across all work-life models are less happy compared to 1972. Money, freedom, education, power, career—the options for women are endless, but has too much choice killed off women's ability to be happy?

The paradox of the multiple-choice society, as described by psychologist Barry Schwartz, is that while we wouldn't want to give it up, having lots of choices doesn't actually seem to make us happy[47]. Nobody wants to go back to the Victorian days of Puritan morals or the suburban perfection of the 1950s. Yet it's tough to deny that women, in their desire to break free and experience it all, have lost sight of how to be happy along the way. We second guess, worry, and worse, live with guilt that we may not be making the best decisions. If we choose to stay at home to care for our children, we worry about wasting our hard-earned education and work experiences. If we commit ourselves to demanding careers, we're tormented that our children may be disadvantaged in some way because we're not physically there for every step.

As a result, we drive ourselves crazy and take away the joys of experiencing whatever choices we have made. We're strung out feeling like we're not doing anything properly and we move farther and farther away from enjoying our choices, taking time for ourselves, and being happy women.

The question is ... can women *choose* to be happy? We are in control of our happiness level to a certain point. In her book *The Myths of Happiness*, Sonja Lyubomirsky demonstrated that 40% of our happiness is by choice. Fifty percent of our happiness is genetically determined, and our job, health, and social status contribute 10% more to our degree of happiness. The factor to focus on is the choice to be happy. Even Abraham Lincoln was quoted as saying, "*Most people are about as happy as they make up their minds to be.*"[48]

How can we choose to be happier? Consider the things in your life and the actions you do that bring a smile to your face and a spark of joy in your heart. Are they part of your daily to-do list? When you consider successes in your life, are they correlated with things that bring you happiness or are they external markers of success?

> When we ask our female clients what makes them happy, the responses are typically

centered around their relationships, feeling good, and a good glass of chardonnay!

These are the type of simple yet impactful joys we want you to factor in when defining success in your life. Being thin, getting the "it" bag of the season, or having the best decorated home in the neighborhood are usually not at the forefront of what makes women happy. Instead, they actually tend to create more anxiety, which in turn becomes the linchpin to unhappiness for women today[49]. We keep striving for things that only give us a temporary happiness fix.

Slowing down and focusing on happiness can create a sense of well-being and becomes just as important to "having your all" as that work promotion. The good news is that many women naturally figure this out as they get older. A Gallup health survey showed that women tend to be happier after the age of 50. They are either in a happy marriage or have left a bad one, gone through menopause, have sent their children off on their own paths, and the pressure to live up to external expectations has diminished[50]. Women at this stage of their lives are defining their lives based on their own needs and desires and end up being happier and at more peace than at any other time of their life.

Gretchen Rubin, author of the *Happiness Project* stated, "The major cause of unhappiness for women in the 21st century is a lack of meaning: too many people climb the perceived ladder of happiness and find it's leaning against the wrong wall. In a manic society, with a lot of external pressures, you're setting yourself up for failure unless you have a well-defined idea of happiness."[51]

So what do happy women look like? We already know that happy people tend to live longer, have better marriages, make more money, are more creative, and have fewer illnesses. But what are some common ingredients in the lifestyle of a happy woman? The following tendencies are compiled from various sources of research. Take a look and see if there might be some things that ring true for you to incorporate into your definition of successful living.

Happy women:

- Understand what makes them personally feel good and turn to these things during challenging times.
- Feel accepted and heard. They stay away from people who make them feel unimportant or unworthy.
- Are less preoccupied with themselves and care more about others (notice the distinction—care about, not care for).
- Get involved in things that are bigger than themselves, whether a campaign, gardening, or their pets.
- Make their own decisions and have a sense of control in their lives—whether to work full-time, part-time, or not at all. Women are happier when they get to choose instead of circumstances choosing for them.
- Want to be themselves—plain and simple, they want to express themselves with freedom from roles and external limitations.
- Like to feel good and be healthy. They tend to engage in physical activities and practice self-care habits.

No one can be happy 100% of the time. Happiness is an immediate and fleeting emotion, sometimes at the whim of things as simple as how our hair looks that day. But the deeper sense of the word is realized through experiencing sustained joy in our lives. Joy is a muscle that can be developed when we no longer look outside of ourselves for approval and instead trust and live from our own internal feelings of contentment.

Throughout this book, we hope to encourage you to take action and define the "all" you want your life to encompass. Your values and passions will provide the backbone to a stronger, healthier, and happier life. Your plate will be filled with healthy habits and things that are valuable to your well-being. If you practice what brings you happiness and sustained joy, you are well on your way to experiencing a fulfilled and contented life—a truly successful way to live!

PART IV

You First!

CHAPTER TEN

Success Through Self-Care

Why self-care? Having your all is about your personal success. No one can take better care of you than you. No one can support you in your success as much as you can. And we believe nothing is more valuable in life than your own health and well-being. Without it, everything we set out to do and accomplish is limited.

The whole premise of this book and the message of our work is that women need to shift their mindset and prioritize and practice self-care in order to achieve their highest success. Since when has stress helped you to be more focused and productive? How helpful is it to go through your day feeling overwhelmed and exhausted? And how much energy do you have in your day with little sleep and poor food choices?

> **It's time to get out of your own way and start putting yourself at the top of your to-do list!**

What is self-care? It's made up of the actions and attitudes that contribute to the maintenance of well-being, personal health, and your own human development. It's making decisions about your lifestyle that will optimally benefit your health and longevity—both physically and mentally. Basically it's all the things you can do that simply feel good and that support your well-being and happiness.

Why then is it so hard for women to choose self-care when it feels so good? Women spend a lot of time making up excuses not to make themselves a priority[52]. Remember, we have a long history of putting the needs of others first. Women worry that taking time for themselves will take time away from others and from extra working hours. We need to change that mindset—doing things for yourself is not self-indulgent or non-productive; it's necessary and ultimately gives you more of an edge by boosting your energy levels to accomplish more of what you really want in your life. It's an investment worth making, which is far from selfish as it supports you and, by default, those with whom you connect.

By engaging in self-care, you assert your right to be your best self. Take a look at the concrete benefits of self-care as demonstrated through research:

Self-Care Benefits to Self	Self-Care Benefits to Corporations
1. Prevents and manages disease	Decreases health care costs
2. Decreases stress and depression	Decreases stress in the workplace
3. Increases immunologic functioning	Decreases sick days
4. Increases capacity for empathy	Increases focus and efficiency
5. Models healthy lifestyle to loved ones	Models healthy behavior in a corporation
6. Enhances friendships and quality of life	Enhances collaboration and teamwork
7. Increases productivity and motivation	Increases work productivity

8. Promotes physical and mental wellbeing	Promotes a healthy environment
9. Lowers feelings of anxiety and worry	Demonstrates that the company values its employees

Self-care is also linked to greater self-reports of happiness and confidence. We all want more of those! Overall, it makes for a more successful person—one that feels balanced, fulfilled, and content, and who is more efficient and productive with their work. Self-care is compassionate care. When taking the time to look after yourself, you are more likely to be able to balance personal activities with professional endeavors and get closer to the elusive work-life balance that we all have been seeking for so long[53].

Can you really have "your" all? Our hope is that by now, we have convinced you that self-care is essential to your success and having "your" all, but how do we get it on our plates? The number one complaint from women today is that they do not have enough time for their self-care and well-being[30]. Since we only have 24 hours in a day and ideally 1/3 of that time would be for sleeping and another third for working, that leaves 8 hours or less for all of our other responsibilities, family, and everything else we need to get done in life. Fitting in self-care comes down to prioritization, and the harder part ... sticking to it!

Prioritization means shifting away from the things you don't have time for and that you really don't even want to do in the first place. You can delegate these tasks, modify them, or get rid of them all together. For example, having to shop for food is one of the biggest complaints of our female clients. It takes a lot of time and there is no getting away from it. Soon after stocking the kitchen, it's time to shop again!

Consider the possibilities: Can you delegate the task to someone else, whether a nanny, spouse, or even an older child? Maybe you can modify your shopping habit to monthly or less frequent visits? How about delivery services or online shopping services? The tasks that frustrate you and take away your energy the most should be your lowest priorities and the ones you find alternative solutions for. You can then use the time savings for self-care activities that benefit your well-being and move you toward your goals. The key is to make self-care a priority. Remember, no more excuses!

Prioritization also means honing in on the self-care strategies that provide the most efficient and the biggest impact to your health and productivity. Look at what you enjoy doing the most and what feels good to your body so that you become both physically and mentally fit. Make up your mind to not only commit to these changes, but also continue to practice and build upon them. We are talking about sustainable, small steps that make you feel good in the moment and that also benefit you long-term as well.

For example, just a small change like getting up a little earlier to head out for a 20-minute power walk in the morning can leave you feeling more focused and energized throughout the day. You'll feel empowered that you started the day in a productive manner, your mood will be elevated from the endorphins flowing through your body, and research indicates that you will be even more likely to make better food choices throughout the rest of that day[54]. Not only does that one small action in the morning benefit you in a variety of ways throughout that morning, but it sets up your body and mind to perform their best throughout the day.

Take a look at the following examples of some of our clients who have made one small self-care change in their life that has yielded some pretty powerful results:

Sophia, a marketing manager, found that simply doing yoga three times a week made her more relaxed, calm, and happy. Her classes were in the evening after long days at work and she found that she was able to let go of her stressors, shut-off her "monkey mind," and sleep so much better at night.

Jennifer is a busy real estate agent with a hectic and varied schedule that left her with either big gaps without eating or eating fast food on the go. Her most effective self-care step was to subscribe to a healthy meals service that delivered a week's worth of meals to her doorstep that she could bring with her to work for quick bites when she was hungry. She is eating healthier (for basically the same cost), has lost weight, and feels re-energized about herself and her work.

Marlene, a principal of an elementary school who spends her days giving her all to others, was looking for a sense of rejuvenation in her life. She formed a hiking club with friends that allows her to spend the weekends exploring new trails in her area. She enjoys getting outdoors and into the fresh air. Being in nature rejuvenates her spirit and gets her ready for the work week.

Sarah is a product manager at a high tech company who was overwhelmed by the number of emails she had to process 24/7 and felt that she could never take a break from thinking about work. She was copied on every e-mail sent between her team members, many of them working globally. We worked with her to create some time-outs in her schedule from 8:00pm onward and after 12:00pm on the weekends so that her team knew she wouldn't be checking in with her work e-mails. If there were urgent issues, they knew to contact her via text. Sarah finally had time in her schedule to balance herself and focus on other parts of life.

These are just a few examples of how one simple step toward well-being can have an incredible impact on your quality of life. It almost sounds too easy, but think back to the small changes you have made in your life in the past and how quickly you were able to see and feel their impact.

Small changes are doable and sustainable, and they build momentum toward bigger goals.

The upcoming *Power Habits* section of the book is filled with additional small steps to fill your plate and turn them into long term habits. It's true ... one small self-care action can be such a powerful catalyst to more of what you want in life.

Remember, taking time for wellness is not a selfish act. It increases your productivity, energy and focus. It allows you to work more efficiently and accomplish more of what you want, therefore benefiting not just yourself but also everyone around you. We have heard it time and again ... put your own oxygen mask on first before helping others. You are able to do more of what you want in life when you take care of yourself first!

CHAPTER ELEVEN
No More Excuses

Meet Roxy, a fictional compilation of many of our female clients who feel stuck with where they are in their lives.

Roxy is in her early 50s with two children out of the house and an executive position that she worked hard for many years to achieve. She has been divorced for five years, and although she has been on a couple of dates, she hasn't put much effort into her self-care or her personal life. She worked hard to get to where she is at with her job. Seemingly, her identity is wrapped around her work and not her health or love life.

Roxy is usually the first one in the office and the last one to leave, as she takes pride in keeping things under control at work. She sits on various volunteer boards through work and is heavily involved with her local and national trade associations. Twice a week she visits her ailing mother who lives in a nearby nursing home and she goes to church on Sunday. Once in awhile, Roxy is able to make it to her Weight Watchers group meeting, of which she is a lifetime member, although most recently her weight has gradually been moving in the opposite direction than the program intends.

She has good relationships with her neighbors and co-workers, but she doesn't spend much time with them socially. Roxy comes home after a long day of working and usually microwaves a Weight Watchers meal, does her household activities, finishes up some work, and then plops down in front of the TV with a bowl of low-fat popcorn before heading to bed an hour later than she probably should.

Every night as she gets ready for bed, Roxy tells herself that she really needs to go to bed earlier, not snack so late, get out to meet more people, pick up some hobbies, go to her Weight Watchers meetings more often, make fresh foods, meet with her friends for some exercise, and work less hours. She knows what she needs to do, but just can't seem to break free from her ingrained habits.

It's now five years later and Roxy is still living the same life and making the same excuses to herself: "I won't snack while watching TV starting tomorrow, on Monday I'll start walking at lunchtime, and I'll work less when we close out the fiscal year next month." The excuses she makes to herself have now become part of her daily routine! Roxy is stuck in a rut of making poor self-care choices. Her actions have become habits and have extinguished the little spark of desire within her to take care of her well-being and live a life full of excitement, fun, growth, and passion.

One day, as Roxy was getting ready for work and about to put on her makeup, she looked directly into the mirror at herself. She stared hard and long and realized that she didn't even recognize the person staring back at her! "This woman before me looks haggardly and sad," she thought. There was no energy in her demeanor, no excitement in her eyes. Roxy did not look like the woman she thought she would be at this stage of her life. Even with all of her career success and the accomplishment of raising two children who were doing well on their own, she felt like a failure.

Obviously Roxy is not feeling very "foxy"! She has made making excuses a pattern in her life and she now has a life that reflects it. We spend a lot of time in that place between "I know I really should do this" and the world of "I'm actually doing it." It's not a knowledge issue, as Roxy has been to so many Weight Watchers meetings she could probably teach the class—yet she's still frustrated with her weight. Inaction, justification, and rationalization are powerful coping mechanisms for a life that feels desperate, out of synch, and even out of control. These excuses, both conscious and subconscious, are faulty reasoning and destructive myths that keep us down and make our lives smaller, less joyful, and less rewarding.

Research shows that when the need to act is the most urgent, subjects dig deep into their habitual excuse patterns more than ever[55]. That's where Roxy found herself, until staring into the mirror made her question her life choices. She knew she was unhappy and dissatisfied with her life. Was she going to pull out her old, tried and true favorite excuses and put them on like old comfy jeans to live out another similar day in her life? Or was she ready to take a step toward something bigger and better? Stay tuned…

In the meantime, let's take a look at what we, as women, are infamous for saying to ourselves, and sadly, believing all too often. The following are the top three excuses the two of us encounter in our work, with our girlfriends, and even between ourselves. We have heard versions of these three "song-and-dance numbers" so many times that it's sad to think how much women could accomplish in the world if they could just get over these infamous excuses.

The first one is the lack of time and with it, its sidekick procrastination. Hands down, not having enough time is the biggest challenge for women trying to do everything they want to do. But we all only have the same 24 hours in each day. It's the great equalizer. So what becomes important is making sure that what you are spending your time on is worth part of those 24 hours.

> **Either you are doing something that moves you toward your goals and represents what is important to you in life, or you are not.**

It may mean that you have to shift priorities, ask for help, or even be creative with how you spend your time. These are all strategies to help you make your time more valuable. Remember, you get to choose what goes on to your plate. Make it worth living or knock it out of your schedule.

Your time is as valuable as you want it to be. We can all be more efficient and productive, but we also need to be more thoughtful with what we spend our time on. That's why it was important to determine what you value, what you are passionate about, and what brings happiness in your life, as we did earlier in the book. That includes self-care, which is time well spent and an investment with unlimited and powerful added returns.

As most women seem to be busy dealing with their overflowing plates, they also may have the tendency to procrastinate. For some reason, "tomorrow" or "later" when "I have more time," when "I finish this other thing," or even when "I feel like doing it" are the most common thoughts that get procrastinators in trouble. Think of what we say to our doctors when they encourage us to make healthier choices—"I know, I should, I will." What is true but never spoken is "just not today"! We might as well be waiting for a blue moon, because there is no better time than right now. The elusive better time never exists, so accepting and prioritizing your self-care will get it off your mental to-do list and straight into action. It will save a lot of guilt and will actually be more likely to get done and benefit your life.

The second most common excuse we hear from our female clients is "I'm not ready" to make the changes I know I need to at this time. "I can't do (fill in the blank) because I'm not (fill in the blank ... organized enough, rich enough, thin enough, etc)." This isn't a procrastination excuse as much as it's waiting for the desire to arise from within. Women sometimes have an "all or nothing" mindset and approach to life. It's that perfectionism mentality that keeps getting us into trouble. "If I can't do it perfectly, then I won't do anything at all"! Many of us tend to be very uncomfortable living within shades of gray. We have patience for our children and co-workers for just doing their best, but we expect the absolute highest standards from ourselves. So we tell ourselves that we're not ready right now and we'll wait until we get "there" and then make changes.

The stark reality is that no one is ever really ready to make changes. We resist change fiercely. We tend to be open to change only when the lives we have created have become so intolerable that we realize that there is no way to overcome it except to move through and beyond it. The way to have an exciting and enriching life is to stretch way out of your comfort zone, stop being afraid of making mistakes, and be okay with walking through the unknown. This takes courage and perseverance, and for most of us, "we just aren't ready"! But you need to throw this excuse out the window because chances are you'll never be perfectly ready. Life is unknown and uncontrollable, so you just need to focus on taking the next step in front of you toward a healthier and more meaningful life. These steps don't have to be giant strides—baby steps are great at building momentum and getting you to where you want to go.

The third biggest and most famous excuse we hear is some version of self-doubt and guilt. This is a little less tangible, but so powerful nonetheless. The internal dialogue that goes on within women's minds is incredible and incredibly crazy! Whether it's learned messaging from our childhood, workplace, relationships, or society, we have made self-doubt and criticism our default thought process. So many successful women today have life-long friendships with their inner critic voice that does nothing but sabotage the positives in their lives.

These thoughts keep us from believing that we are worthy and deserving of an amazing life and that we have what it takes to create it. We tend to minimize our enormous capabilities, talents, and gifts that can be of service to others and the world. But remember, you are not your thoughts! Anything you think and feel can be changed.

> **If you're unhappy and dissatisfied with your life, this isn't just "you"; this is a version of you that you can modify.**

It doesn't matter who you are and what your life experiences and history have been, you have something special to offer to this world and you have to get out of your own way to be able to share it.

Guilt has an important role in feeding the fierce flames of our self-doubt. Forget putting ourselves first, it's tough for women to put ourselves as a higher priority than our families, work, our social commitments, service obligations, and even housecleaning!

> **Repeat after us ...**
> **self-care is not selfish!**

When you treat yourself with some kindness and respect, good things trickle down to all the other areas of your life—your home and work life, your relationships, and your community. Yes, your children and work are a priority, but you deserve to be a priority, too. Your ability to take care of others is directly proportional to your own sense of vitality and happiness.

Spending money on life goals or your self-care also tends to create guilty feelings. Don't make guilt the reason you don't go after what you want in life. Empower yourself to find some ways around it and go after solutions rather than playing the victim role. A little investment in yourself reinforces the message that you, your time, and your energy are valuable. Your well-being is a great investment with a fabulous short-term and long-term pay-off!

Guilt is also an emotion that covers up the fear of disapproval. What if other people comment or judge us for making ourselves a priority? Ladies, whose disapproval are we avoiding? Instead of feeling guilty, we need to embrace a more individualistic and self-reliant view of life. The world is filled with judgmental, negative, and critical people who are ready and willing to contribute to our self-doubt. Misery loves company, and it's usually this type of group mentality that keeps us continuously doing in life what makes us miserable. Trust in yourself and hold on strongly to the belief that you have the right and the worthiness to live your life as you dream it. Don't let guilt and the naysayers hold you back!

So, what's your excuse? What are the thoughts and beliefs in your mind that keep you from achieving your potential and living with fulfillment? Take a look at the checklist below compiled from a variety of sources and check off what sounds familiar. Are your excuses greater than your dreams?

WOMEN'S TOP EXCUSES:

- I don't have the knowledge/certification/credentials.
- I can't get the education required.
- I don't know the right people.
- I don't have the money.

No More Excuses!

- I can't afford to take the risk right now.
- It's too hard.
- I don't learn that way.
- Somebody else is already doing that.
- I don't know where to begin.
- I'm afraid of what my colleagues will say.
- Nobody will care.
- It's better to be safe than sorry.
- I haven't done this before.
- I'm not that good at it.
- I'm not a lucky person.
- My gender won't let me.
- My kids are my first priority.
- My spouse won't like it.
- My health won't let me.
- It's not financially sound.
- The ROI (Return On Investment) is unclear.
- The market conditions aren't right.
- There's no point.
- I'll get to it later.
- I'm not ready for that level of success.
- I don't like what success did to (fill in the blank).
- I may not be able to handle the extra responsibilities.
- I'm afraid of failing.
- I have too many things on my plate.
- I'm not creative enough.
- I'm a better thinker than a doer.

- There are too many obstacles in the way.
- I've tried before and failed.
- I don't want to spend too much time away from family.
- I don't have the space and quiet I need to get things done.
- I'm always just too tired.
- I just can't stop doing (fill in the unproductive habit).
- I'm not confident enough.
- I'm not a natural leader.
- I don't like public speaking.
- I don't have a good support system.
- I don't want to start something I may not be able to finish.
- My friends/family will think I'm crazy.
- What will other people think?
- It's too selfish.
- I don't deserve it.
- I do enough already.
- The timing is not right.
- I don't work well with a team.
- I'm too old.
- I'm too young.
- I'm not good at (fill in the blank).
- I don't have time.
- _____(Add in your favorite excuse.)

How many excuses did you check off? How many of them are part of your daily life? Some are easy to recognize as cop-outs, but many make us feel righteous for sacrificing our own needs for others. Those are the tough excuses to stop using because they require us to put our needs higher up on the priority list. But ask those you are making sacrifices for and see how they feel about your choices. You may be surprised with what you learn.

Think through the situations that make you unsatisfied in your life and consider why you haven't made changes or explored different options. Are you in the middle of a mid-life crisis, not for fear of getting old since you knew that was coming, but like Roxy, fearing the realization that who you are and who you thought you would be at this stage of your life doesn't match up? If so, this may be an opportunity to re-evaluate and forge a healthier path in your life.

Remember, you can have results or excuses, but not both!

CHAPTER TWELVE
Get Your Groove On

Even though we have learned so much over the past 75 years within the field of behavior change, we still struggle as a society in making lasting changes compared to choices that yield short-term benefits. Both of us have seen this over and over again with our clients. We know it's much tougher and more complicated to help them make meaningful changes compared to just educating them on work-life balance or what the benefits of food choices and exercise are. We all struggle with making habits stick, but the pay-offs are worth the effort once we allow ourselves to explore change. Remember, you get to choose what and how much goes on to your plate. If it doesn't make you happy or get you to your goals, you have the ability to change it.

Once you know the direction you want to move toward in life through defining your personal version of success, the next thing is to actually take that first step forward. Breaking out of ruts requires steering into a different direction and willingness to shift into a different gear. It doesn't have to be more complicated than that. We are encouraging you to move toward a life where your well-being is a priority. That doesn't mean a set prescription on how to live, but instead moving you toward your personal version of successful living that feels good and is meaningful to you.

So if something is not working, change it! That sounds so simple, but we make it so tough when we keep the tape playing of our favorite excuses. We end up staying in places that are comfortable and we let fear get in the way of making changes. And what happens when we don't let ourselves evolve and make changes over time? Our comfort zone keeps on getting smaller and smaller as our fears of anything outside of it continue to grow[56]. It's no wonder that we maintain such a strong grip on our comfortable, yet unproductive ways.

Do we actually need the infamous 21 days to be able to break and form a new habit? We struggle to find an extra 10 minutes in our day, how are we going to find 21 days for each and every change we want to make in our lives? Welcome to our "go as slow as you need to go, but go" version of change management! We know from research that it's never too late to create new healthy habits and we do not need an official 21 days to do it[57]. Just don't make it more complicated than it needs to be and let's throw those excuses that are exhausting us out the window.

Habits are malleable throughout life, but the best way to change a habit is to understand its structure. A simple explanation is that habits break down into cues, routines, and rewards. Most people emphasize the routine, but if you actually target the cues that spark the behavior and the reward it provides, the behavior can be more easily modified[57].

For example, in Roxy's life, a change she would like to make is avoiding overeating in front of the TV when she's not hungry. This habit makes it difficult for her to manage her weight and she doesn't feel good about herself by the time she drags herself up from the couch to go to bed. Maybe the cue or trigger for Roxy is that she's coming home to an empty home and that she is really tired and just wants some comfort after a long day. So she plops down in front of the TV with a big bowl of popcorn every night and watches mindless TV, which signals that she is finally done with her day. She's not even hungry and she doesn't really enjoy what she's watching, but she feels depleted after a long day and probably a little lonely now that she doesn't have anyone to share her evenings with. Popcorn and the TV are her new best friends that give her the comfort she's looking for.

Roxy now has to find a different routine that still provides her with this same feeling of comfort for her reward. What can she do? Maybe Roxy stops buying popcorn and instead drinks a cup of hot tea and reads in her bedroom, which she loves to do but has given up on because she didn't think she had enough time. Drinking a hot cup of herbal tea is relaxing for her since she has to sip it slowly, and reading is a treat for her since she told herself she didn't have time in her life to read.

Roxy now heads straight to her favorite cozy chair in her bedroom as her new cue, where she picks up her book and avoids her old cue of the TV in the living room seductively calling out to her to join her for the night. She now goes to bed earlier, as she is content with reading a few chapters before listening to her body tell her that she's done for the day. She ends her day feeling good about herself because she is being more productive with what's meaningful to her and less destructive with mindless habits.

Our brains are programmed to create habits around behaviors that deliver a reward. Roxy is now even thinking about joining a book club to add a little more purpose to her reading and to bring more social activities back into her life as a long-term reward. In the meantime, Roxy is feeling much more "foxy" as she is looking and feeling so much better with proper sleep, an end to her nighttime mindless eating, and her new positive feelings about herself and her life. You go, Roxy!

Now, if only it was as easy as herbal tea and a good book! We know that was only one change Roxy made in her life and that she has other areas of her life that she might want to make changes in as well. While we all enjoy shining moments of accomplishments in our lives, we also struggle with multiple challenging aspects of ourselves. Change is good but it can also be time consuming and energy draining.

So we have created our own "CHANGE IS GOOD Cheat Sheet" filled with strategies and tips to help streamline your success and get you to where you want to go. This is by no means a comprehensive list, but is filled with the tools we use with our clients to help move them from destructive and harmful habits to self empowering ones. Take a look ... you have our permission to cheat!

CHANGE IS GOOD CHEAT SHEET

- **Start small and then go big.** When you're trying to make changes in your life, start smaller than small. You can always go bigger as you build your confidence and determine what works well for you. Start with a change that takes almost no time and very minimal effort. For example, a study of postmenopausal women demonstrated that women who set small goals like increasing exercise sessions in five-minute increments did better at the end of the two-year study compared to the control group who had adapted quickly to a full-exercise program only to abandon it later[58].

- **One thing at a time.** Focus on one change at a time. It's challenging enough to make one change; it's even tougher if you have to divide your time and energy to take on multiple changes all at once.

- **Piggyback for success.** Let your new habit hitch a ride on to an existing and established action that you already do. For example, doing it right after a task that is established in your routine will help as a reminder compared to creating a new time and space into your day.

- **Create, don't break.** Focus on developing positive habits versus trying to end old ones. Breaking habits is a psychology experiment of its own. Instead, create a new habit that makes it difficult to do an old one. For example, we like to encourage our stressed and exhausted clients who tend to mindlessly eat at night, like Roxy, to end their day with a hot shower. It relaxes them, which is what they really need, and you can't eat while you're in the shower, so it easily breaks the old habit while creating one that actually solves the problem.

- **Get out of town.** Changing a habit while on vacation is one of the most successful ways to kick-start change. All of your old cues and old reward systems aren't in your environment anymore, so you have the ability to form new patterns more effectively. The challenge is to be able to carry over the changes into your daily life upon return. Starting something after taking a break and with fresh eyes is a great way to get a jumpstart.

- **Practice.** Try to repeat the action five times when you first attempt a new action. This will help establish it as a normal action that feels familiar and adds a sense of comfort to doing something new.
- **Sunrise or Sunset.** Morning and evening actions seem to be more effective than actions done in the middle of the day. Exercise is a perfect example of this. It's much more likely that you will get in a short bout of movement at the beginning of your day before showering compared to expecting yourself to leave work midday, change, exercise, shower, and go back to work. It has to make sense with your schedule.
- **Celebrate!** Reward yourself every time you complete a new action. You want to affirm that you did something positive toward making changes. Self-celebrate with a fist bump in the air, do your happy dance, or tell yourself that you rock—the emotional impact of the celebration helps seal in the action. Your brain feels happy and excited and will start to make a positive connection with the job well done as it becomes more of a habit[59].
- **Face forward.** No matter how fast or slow your progress is taking you, you need to keep yourself moving in the direction of growth. Part of being human is the experience of always being a work in progress. There will be times when life is cooperating and everything is working well to support your changes, and there will be times when you aren't able to follow through with your plans. The key is to stand still if you need to during the difficult times, but not let yourself fall into a downward spiral back to where you started from. It's okay to stay in a plateau until you can move forward once again, but it's tough to relapse back and forth between success and failure. Protect your movement forward no matter what. Remember that you are dropping your "all or nothing" thinking once and for all!
- **It's time to come clean.** One of the biggest challenges we face is being around the same unsupportive environments that are filled with triggers and cues for our old, unwanted behaviors. Controlling your environment will be essential for your success. There are too many reminders and too much dependence on willpower if you

don't adjust, modify, or clean out your surroundings. That may mean something simple like cleaning out the foods that call your name (trigger foods) from your home, or it may even mean ending toxic relationships that are not supportive to who you want to be and your having "your" all.

- **Go inside.** Before you embark on making changes in your life or if you hit some roadblocks along the way, you may need to address any lingering internal conflicts that are making it difficult for you to move forward. You should be clear and specific on why you want to change. Your inner motivations form the intrinsic drive that moves you into action and ultimately changes you for the better. Try to fully understand the results of making changes and the consequences of not making changes. Get help if you need it because you may just have to defeat your own worst enemy first, which is yourself.

- **Make it easy for yourself.** In our work, we find creating defaults one of the most effective ways to work with the busy schedules and cognitive overload of our professional clients. Defaults simplify and guide decisions by making it easier to choose one action (the default) and harder to choose another[60]. For example, in trying to fit fitness into busy schedules, strategies like participating in early morning boot camp classes at a gym near work that has shower facilities is a much easier choice than sitting in rush hour traffic going to work. Committing to walking with a co-worker at lunchtime means showing up is much easier than having to come up with excuses as to why you can't join her and deal with the guilt of bowing out. Establishing default structures within your schedule is a creative way to get the job done and it makes it more painful to opt out. In time, new healthy habits are developed and the decision anxiety that you might have faced with knowing you should do something, but not wanting to do it, is eliminated. Voila!

- **Share and share often.** Set yourself up for success by putting yourself around positive, uplifting, and supportive people. Share with them your wins, joys, and celebrations for added motivation, and team up for even more accountability. Research from Brown

University showed that those who lost weight or made other changes in their behavior seemed to get lots of encouragement from friends, family, and co-workers and especially from those attempting similar changes in their lives[61].

- **Get tech help.** The mobile-health field, the growing number of apps, and self-monitoring gadgets and gizmos are making it much easier to take on behavior change and preventive health in fun and convenient ways. Behavioral technology allows you to gradually alter all kinds of behavior and all from the convenience of your smart phone. Take advantage of the convenience and have some fun at the same time!

The key is to pick one of these strategies and apply it to a change you want to make in your life. If it is helpful, continue to practice it and begin to create a new routine and rhythm that displaces something that isn't working as well for you. As we explore the *5 Power Habits* together, you will begin to notice the specific self-care actions that will support living your life to its fullest. Integrate the "Change Is Good Cheat Sheet" strategies to transform these actions into true habits—and get empowered for lasting change!

CHAPTER THIRTEEN

Get Ready, Mind Set, Go!

We have covered a lot of ground in this book and are now headed toward the exciting how-to's for leading energized, empowered, and effective lives! Before we dive into the" take action" section with our *5 Power Habits*, it's important to spend some time making sure you develop a concrete mindset for effectuating change. You have thrown out your excuses and are ready to create some new moves in your lives, but let's make sure you are setting yourself up to succeed in a consistent and repeatable manner. Most women have making changes on their minds, but they approach it in a haphazard manner where the outcomes end up being varied and they are left feeling frustrated and less confident. No more of that ... let's get you prepped for success!

When we reflect back on all the clients we have worked with that have been successful in making meaningful changes in their lives, there are three traits these clients exhibit that stand out as being essential to achieving their goals: **clarity, optimism, and resilience.** These are three important qualities that can get you through the hurdles and challenges that pop up as you move toward your self-care goals.

This little trio of qualities can help push you past both your comfort zone and your current abilities to help you take charge of your life. The goal is to not allow circumstances to take control of you, but rather mentally enable you to take control of circumstances. The more you cultivate these three traits within yourself, the more they are going to help you get from where you are today to where you want to be in life, while hopefully enjoying the journey along the way. So, let's dive in and get going!

1. CLARITY

> *"The truth about women and power is that people think we have it, but we don't—because we are not using it. Every woman must think this through for herself; everyone must embark on her own voyage of discovery. There are no guarantees that you'll be successful, or that you'll be loved, but if you have a vision and if you have the courage to pursue it, you can achieve a wonderful and meaningful life."*
>
> HARRIETT WOODS,
> FORMER PRESIDENT OF THE NATIONAL WOMEN'S POLITICAL CAUCUS

We love this message … have a vision and the courage to pursue it. If you want to go somewhere, be clear about where you want to go and create a plan on how to get there. Be steadfast and strong and then go! We'll get to the courage aspect in a bit when we talk about resilience, but let's start with having the clarity to really know what you want.

Remember what we discovered in the beginning of the book—it's what **you** want on your plate, it's **your** definition of success, and it's **your** having it all. No need to wait for someone else's approval, direction, or permission. You're not going after any "shoulds" or what your boss, mother, spouse, or other external influencers want from you. You can't let non-essential thoughts, worries, and excuses derail you from your intentions. They just get in the way of your productivity, concentrating on what really matters, and what you need to get done right now.

It's not easy, we know. Women are so used to multi-tasking that it's almost too difficult to stay focused on one thing at time. The "monkey mind" described in yoga class is a perfect example of how we go through our days. How many thoughts and to-do's creep into your mind that you really can't do anything about in that moment? You can't run out to pick up groceries or dress for the event coming up or return the phone call that you are thinking about while you are in downward facing dog and being reminded to breathe. All you can do is be focused on the task at hand, be present in the moment, and have clarity about your intentions.

2. OPTIMISM

A second trait we tend to see in our successful clients is having a positive attitude. "I think I can" will beat out "I can't" every time. Being optimistic means having a hopeful, positive outlook about yourself, your future, and the world around you. It's a flexible frame of mind that accepts change as growth and is ready to adjust to it.

It's also a conscious decision to choose attitudes and behaviors that lead toward your own happiness. It's putting yourself in environments and around people that support your feeling joy. Who wouldn't choose those, right? Well, remember where women have come from over the years. Our major responsibilities have been to make other people happy and to support the success of others, like our spouses and children. Now it's time for us to reprogram our beliefs and choose attitudes and actions that dictate our own happiness and success in life.

The women who are able to embrace optimism are the ones who are not only getting to where they want to go, but they're getting there with a smile on their face. How successful does irritated, negative, and grumpy look? Don't let yourself go there!

By definition, optimism lets you see, feel, and think positively. Don't worry if you weren't born a natural "Pollyanna"—not many of us were. It's a trait, however, that we can practice and develop to gradually become our default outlook with proven returns of engagement and performance in the workplace[62]. It's not just expecting the best and hoping that things will go well, though. In daily life, or when faced with a crisis, it's _choosing_ to look at things with a positive viewpoint and making the most of what life brings your way. Remember the popular saying to make "lemonade out of lemons"? Well, we are telling women to take those sour lemons that life hands us and stuff them into our bras!

3. RESILIENCE

Whether you think you can or you think you can't, you're right! Might as well go for it and get what you want out of life with as much perseverance and commitment as you can. That's resilience! It's overcoming challenges and turning them into opportunities. It's being proactive and not giving up when the going gets tough.

Working through challenging experiences and failures enables you to uncover talents you may not have known you had. You might make a mistake or get a bad break, but you bounce back as quickly as you can and keep facing and moving forward. You are able to build self-reliance from these challenges and the experience of problem-solving and getting through tough times[63]. Giving up, making excuses, or letting your spirit be defeated is always an option, but it's also the easy way out.

Resilience is also an essential strength for women in order to overcome some of the traditional gender obstacles that still linger in the workplace. It builds your confidence to cope with whatever life throws at you, whether personally, socially, or professionally. Regardless of the situation, it will never stay forever bleak or forever positive, so building resilience helps give you a balanced perspective in life.

For example, one of the toughest challenges you can experience is facing an unexpected and many times uncontrollable illness. Sheer will-power and self-discipline are not enough to get through this type of adversity. Resilience is about riding the wave and not fighting the reality, using your time and energy in places where you can actually make a difference. When you keep yourself in the big picture of life, you are building your ability to take on the bumps of life and come out stronger and wiser

Regardless of what kind of success you are seeking, remember that you are the one responsible for getting yourself there. We are giving you the practical tips and tools to help get you there with the upcoming *Power Habits,* but having clarity, an optimistic attitude, and resilience can be the boosters that can get you there even faster. So, get ready, get set, and let's go!

PART V

The 5 Power Habits

CHAPTER FOURTEEN

It's Time to Power Up!

Why the 5 *Power Habits* **and where did they come from?** As we worked with women to improve their health and lifestyles in our consulting businesses, we were able to see how effective wellness and self-care habits were in helping to transform women's lives. Women wanted to feel *energized*, they want to be *empowered* in their life choices, and they wanted to be *effective* in how they lead their lives ... and we wanted to get them there! We began to develop the basis of the book around what actions would help women feel the most energized, empowered, and effective.

- What actions had the biggest impact on women's health?
- What habits were the most effective in helping our clients achieve their goals?
- What was being discovered in the latest research on work-life fit and wellness?
- What were the self-care practices we, as health experts, relied on the most?
- What needs to be in our lives in order for us to have our all?

We determined that there were 5 key areas of life observed in our most happy, successful, and healthiest clients. These five areas of life, which we called the *5 Power Habits*, represent the most universal areas of wellness research and the most effective habits for maximizing well-being. Most exciting of all, we found that when our clients integrated these 5 aspects of self-care into their lives, they were able to not only optimize their health and productivity, but also their level of overall life satisfaction. Utilizing the 5 Power Habits gave them more energy, contributed to their self-empowerment, and helped them be more effective in getting what they needed to get done.

We also learned that no two women are the same, and therefore we need to have a variety of options for women to choose from. Each of us comes with our own medical and personal histories, and we all have a long list of behavior changes we have attempted in the past. Some strategies may have worked well and some may not have been a good fit for our personalities or lives. This book does not contain a structured plan or rigid system to follow; instead, it encourages you to choose the actions that work with your lifestyle and your needs. You can choose and practice them based on what is most realistic for you and that can be sustainable in the long run.

We also believe that busy women want things fast and like things to be spelled out easily. As a result, the idea of highlighting our top 10 list of actions under each *Power Habit* took shape to save you time and energy and maximize the potential for your success.

The 5 Power Habits are not about piling on more tasks in your life—instead you can choose which specific actions speak to you the most. You may decide to pick only one specific action within one *Power Habit* such as "move," or maybe you are ready to take on several actions from all *5 Power Habits*. Start with considering which actions you may have tried in the past that worked and determine which actions sound interesting, fun, and realistic.

Don't be scared off by adding something new to your plate! Making yourself a priority does not have to change your comfortable routines overnight. Nor does taking care of yourself mean that you have to ignore your other responsibilities. Self-care does not demand sudden and big shifts. We encourage making an impact through small changes. Sometimes the smallest and simplest choices create the largest and most significant results because they are sustainable and they fit with your personality and lifestyle. Remember, there is no magic bullet or pill for self-care.

Introducing the *Power Habits*—our 5 pillars of wellbeing: Purpose, Balance, Rejuvenation, Move, and Nourish. These 5 components support your self-care and provide a platform to live your most successful life. We encourage you to make room on your plates for them and let them lead you to more energized, empowered, and effective living!

The 5 POWER HABITS

PURPOSE: integrates concepts from positive psychology and supports exploring and living a life based on what is meaningful to you.

BALANCE: creates a lifestyle that minimizes stress and promotes harmony in all areas of life.

REJUVENATE: encourages adequate rest, connection, simple joys, and fun in life.

MOVE: includes activities for feeling and looking your best—both inside and out.

NOURISH: fosters mindful and balanced eating habits for optimal energy and health.

There you have it—our high five of self-care! It's not overly complicated, yet how many of you would say you experience or engage in these areas on a regular basis? We all have our well-planned days and our "fly be the seat of our pants" days, but when you focus on creating habits around these areas, you begin to create a lifestyle that supports your health, productivity, well-being, and, we would argue—"having your all"!

We encourage you to connect to these 5 areas of self-care and reflect on how present they are in your life right now. Which ones are you practicing consistently and are part of your daily routines, and which ones do you need more of in the future? Overall, the *5 Power Habits* allow you to gain control of your time and energy, and they enable you to focus on the things that are critical to your definition of success. They support what you value, are passionate about, and what brings fulfillment to your life—both at work and home.

Bringing the *Power Habits* to life. Mid-career and mid-life is a time that many women tend to re-evaluate and reflect on what really matters to them most. It is a prime phase of life when titles and material possessions start to take a back seat to what really may matter to them—for example, relationships, health, and purpose[64].

Meet Jessie, a client who falls in this category:

Jessie is in her late 50s and works as a full-time bank executive. She gets up at 6am for her outdoor fitness class, a workout that consists of running, a ropes course, and weight training. An hour after her class, Jessie is feeling anything but the fatigue of a tough workout—she is jazzed up and ready to take on a fresh new day! What she loves about this workout is starting her day outside in nature, be it rain or shine. The comraderie of group exercise and the variety keeps Jessie motivated and coming back.

Since her work is close to home, Jessie also often takes a quick lunch break to walk her dog and grab her lunch of healthy leftovers. On days she has to meet with clients for lunch, she chooses from a handful of local restaurants that she knows provide healthy options. On those days, her secret to grabbing a jog with the dog the minute she comes home from a long day is the workout tank she wears as an under layer to her work blouse. This makes it easy to be ready to head out and not get caught up in other things when she comes home.

Jessie's life was not always so. As a high-level executive, Jessie often found herself working such long hours that by Friday she just wanted to spend her weekends recuperating on the couch with lots of comfort food. Since focusing on the one action of adding more movement into her life, Jessie has also been able to reignite her passion for the outdoors and gain from the social interactions of her "Exercise Peers." That one simple step of signing up for the fitness class has brought so many positives to her life.

It's Time to Power Up!

It's amazing how simple yet powerful taking care of yourself can be. This book presents many ideas and strategies for self-care. You can choose to do nothing at all or you can choose to go for it all! We just ask you to consider what your life looks like right now and then consider what your life would look like with more purpose, balance, rejuvenation, movement, and nourishment.

Change isn't something that can be simply handed to someone; it's a state we have to be ready for. That's why it's essential to understand what you value and what motivates you to foster change. If Roxy, who you met earlier in the book, never looked at herself in the mirror, where would her life and health be right now? Where is yours headed?

Like a Vegas buffet, you will be able to choose which 5 Power Habits and their wisdom goes on your plate and which ones in particular suit you and your lifestyle goals. So grab a plate because the Power Habit buffet is now officially open and it's time to move from being an *exhausted* woman to becoming an *energized, empowered,* and *effective* woman!

THE POWER OF PURPOSE

> *The purpose of life is to live it, to taste experience to the utmost, to reach out eagerly and without fear for newer and richer experience.*
>
> ELEANOR ROOSEVELT

As the owner of a large private practice, Sarah found herself working more hours than she wanted to. Even with a supportive family and fulfilling profession, Sarah's life was missing a feeling of passion and excitement. Sarah is naturally creative and observant, and as a child she remembered earning a photography badge in Girl Scouts. We encouraged her to dust off her camera and bring back some of the fun she used to experience by taking pictures. Sarah started off with a few classes and eventually won a National Photo Magazine Cover Competition. Today, always with a camera nearby, her photos are a great reminder of the other dimensions in her life and of her talents outside of her job. "Taking pictures grounds me, *energizes* me, and *empowers* me to try new things and challenge myself creatively both at work and in play," she says. "My purpose in life is clear and involves tapping into my values and passions and to what matters to me most."

Scratching The Itch

Imagine you are celebrating your 100th birthday and you had time to review your last century! Would you be happy with your life? Or would you wish it had gone differently? The truth is you cannot control all the circumstances in your life, but you can be responsible for creating the life you lead. Grab a pen and paper and take some time to answer these soul searching questions.

- **Look back.** Start by looking into your childhood—a time when you had some great ideas. Perhaps you wanted to be a famous singer or a rocket scientist? Write down what was appealing to you about these jobs. If a singer, did you love music, get energized by performing in front of people, love to hear the roar of applause from the audience? If a rocket scientist, was it the adventure of heading into the unknown, the calculations and design of the rocket itself, or the fascination with physics and numbers? These skills and strengths can be weeded out and woven into a new tapestry. Your new tapestry may not be the exact job or the life you imagined, but it can contain parts of it. Look back now and list what you imagine you would be when you grew up, and with each dream make another sub-list of skills and strengths you can build on for your future.

- **Have no regrets.** Here are six questions you can ask yourself about your life so you do not have any regrets. These questions are based on the *Top Five Regrets of The Dying*, a book by Bronnie Ware.
    1. Are you fulfilling your dreams? What are your dreams?
    2. Do you have courage to live a life true to yourself and not what others expect of you?
    3. Do you work too hard? What about spending more time with people you truly care about? Are you spending enough time on projects and hobbies that energize you?

4. Do you harbor resentment or bitterness? Are you true to your feelings? Are your feelings holding you back from your highest potential? Essentially, are you in the way of you?

5. Have you stayed in touch with old friends? When was the last time you called, Skyped, visited, or connected to each other?

6. Are you true to yourself? When was the last time you had a good laugh, were silly, or just showed up as your authentic self?

- **<u>Remember you.</u>** When your life is over, how do you want people to remember you? What would you want your dearest friends and family to say about you at your funeral? Dare to reflect and write this down.

- **<u>Three soul searching questions for continued journaling.</u>**

    1. What five things are you most proud of?
    2. How do you want to leave the world a better place?
    3. What five things do you want to achieve before you die?

With intention, you can move toward your goals. Bit by bit you will be able to look back upon your life and feel it was well spent.

Finding Flow

Flow is described as reaching your highest element of enjoyment combined with a challenge. An example of flow is when you run a marathon, play music, or become immersed in a book. In flow, you reach a point where everything feels effortless and there is no distinction between thought and action, self and environment. A Gallup Poll shows that in the US 15-20% of adults never experience flow, 60-70% experience flow once a week or every few months, and 10-25% of the US population experience flow every day. Here are some suggestions to get more flow in your life.

- **Have clear goals.** Make sure you know what you want to accomplish. Is your goal to finish the marathon or half of the painting?
- **Be aware.** When you are in flow, feedback is immediate. Listen to your body in the moment.
- **Provide a balance between opportunity and capacity.** In other words, match your skills to the activity at hand and make sure there is a level of challenge in the experience you choose.
- **Turn on your brain.** Be willing to deeply concentrate.
- **Become present.** Focus just on the task at hand without interruptions. Don't fight it by checking your clock, checking e-mail, or allowing any other distractions.
- **Let go of all control.** Make sure to enjoy the process (the journey). This could be through work, a hobby, or through exercise. Leave your ego behind and simply enjoy by making sure the experience is interesting to you.

Flow describes maximum enjoyment with maximum achievement and can markedly increase your quality of life. *Psychologist Mihaly Csikszentmihalyi, author of Flow, describes flow as "Being completely involved in an activity for its own sake. The ego falls away. Time flies. Every action, movement, and thought follows inevitably from the previous one, like playing jazz. Your whole being is involved, and you're using your skills to the utmost."* He adds, *"To be successful you have to enjoy doing your best while at the same time contributing to something beyond yourself."*

Record what activities bring you flow or have the potential to:

1. _____
2. _____
3. _____

Pull out your calendar and schedule time to practice these experiences on a regular basis.

Discover Joy In Every Day

The difference between joy and happiness is that happiness is a fleeting emotion, mostly external, while joy is rooted in a deeper feeling. Grabbing that first cup of coffee or tea in the morning makes you happy, but playing the guitar with your band can bring you joy. Here are some exercises to help you find more joy.

- **5 questions to help you discover what makes you feel joyful.**
    1. What are you good at? What activities use your strengths?
    2. What hobbies have you always wanted to pursue?
    3. What sections of a bookstore or library do you navigate toward?
    4. What would you do even if you were not getting paid to do it?
    5. If you only had a short time to live, one year for example, how would you spend that time?

- **Feeling alive.** Is there a time in your life where you felt totally happy and alive? For example, one client replied, *"I can remember running into the ocean in a small village overseas with my best friend as our children and husbands sat aghast on the shore. We laughed so hard at our spontaneity, all the while swimming under the magical clear blue moonlit sky."* From that story we can tell that what makes her feel alive is being spontaneous, the outdoors, travel, and friends.

- **15 minutes of nothing.** Martha Beck, the famous life coach and regular writer in *Oprah* magazine, encourages us to vacate our life for 15 minutes every day. Take a break each day and go somewhere where there are no interruptions. She advises to do something that does not require attention, such as walking, driving, listening to waves crash against the shore, lighting a candle, or just sitting quietly. Let thoughts float through your mind and out of it. Taking this time to do nothing and focus will clear your head and allow you to feel more content.

- **Discover desire.** Desire is such a powerful word. Many of us go through an entire lifetime not knowing or honoring our desires. Your desires can be as simple as taking time on the weekend to hike or bike, or simply planning a dream vacation on a budget. What you desire can be written out in the form of a "Bucket List." Here is your chance now to write down your first five desires that come to mind. Make sure they foster feelings of joy as you record them and feel free to write down what you may consider crazy and outlandish! My top five desires are…

1. _____
2. _____
3. _____
4. _____
5. _____

Finding joy means tapping into your inner peace and appreciating life's bounty. Joy is always available to you, you just have to actively seek it out and practice it.

Get Creative

"Oh, I'm not creative" or "I don't have a creative bone in my body" is hogwash. Everyone is born with creativity. Those who happen to be most creative have enjoyed tapping into it with encouragement and then enjoyed the practice of it. You do not have to be Picasso or Shakespeare—just be willing to try without preconceived judgment. You never know what you can create if given the chance! Here are some tips to get those creative juices flowing.

- **Crafty corners!** Head to a craft store and look for projects to do. With just $50 discover what is there for you to make. Jewelry, paper crafts (stamping, card making, and décor), painting, craft kits, wood projects, doll making, and framing are just a few options.

- **Get messy.** Allow you and your kids to get down-right messy. Stop worrying about getting a cracked egg in the recipe bowl without any shell, the play dough on the carpet, or the paint on the wall. Set up your space to be able to tackle those mishaps. Put down newspaper or old towels, and don aprons or old t-shirts. Getting creative is about getting free and sometimes that involves getting down and dirty.

- **Creativity in the library.** Stuck on projects for kids or yourself? Head to the library and spend an entire afternoon looking through the gardening section, self-help books, crafts, and travel areas. Don't forget to venture into the children's area to discover that this year you may be making those Halloween costumes, even if for you!

- **D.I.Y.** "Do It Yourself" projects are all over the internet. These projects are fun to buy for and fun to create. Give the following items a makeover: an old lamp, an accent wall, your bathroom (stage it with luxury items and plush towels). Learn to knit, make paper crafts, or sew a pillow for your living room. Pinterest online will also give you many DIY ideas to work with.

- **Look at something from a different angle.** Think creatively by merging two unlikely ideas together. What about using wire to sculpt or serving soup in small cups for appetizers? Think about a project by adding an unlikely angle to it.

- **Add creativity at work.** Add poetry to your next work presentation. Draw your ideas out. Add stickers and stamps to scrapbooks and journals or even your meeting documents. For example, Zappos has one of its 10 core company values as being: "Create fun and a little weirdness," and Google believes, "You can be serious without a suit."

- **Generate creative thinking time.** The most creative thoughts for people occur while they are driving, are in the shower, or during exercise. Have a notebook handy to capture your thoughts on paper. Whitespace or time in between scheduled events also leaves room for creative thinking.

Think left, think right, and think low and think high. Oh the thinks you can think up if only you try.

DR. SEUSS

Authentic Self

Being authentic has everything to do with how you were created to be and not what society or the world wants you to be. As we have explored in the beginning of the book, knowing your values helps define what you care about most. Visualizing your goals, discovering your strengths, living the life you design, and learning from the past all help with knowing the real you—a.k.a. your authentic self.

- **Create a vision board**. Having a visual trigger can be inspirational and provide a motivational reminder of where you are now and where you would like to go. Get out those old magazines, paper, scissors, and glue sticks and create a visual collage. Cut out and paste your inspirations and goals onto a board. If your ambition is to spend more time with the family, cut out pictures of family activities that inspire you. If you want to reach a higher level of fitness, cut out images of people who are doing what you would like to do, even add equipment you see yourself wearing, a clock to represent barriers like time—anything to remind you of ways to achieve this goal. Include words as well on your vision board. Don't forget to hang your vision board where you can see it to be reminded of your big goals.

- **Know your top strengths.** Working in your strengths zones allows for maximum productivity and fulfillment. Strengthfinders 2.0 by Tom Rath is a great way to discover what your top five strengths are. At the end of this book is a code to take the online Stengthsfinders quiz. From your results of the quiz you will be able to see what you do best. This book is invaluable not just for yourself as a mid-career working woman, but also for working in teams and knowing how staff and organizations best function.

- **Live by design.** If you were to be stripped of your job, your roles, and what the world expects of you, you would be left with your authentic self. Skills, talents, and wisdom are those elements that are left to describe you at your core. Do you live a life designed by you? Do you use your skills, talents, and wisdom every day?

- **Learn from the past.** Write down what type of work brings you happiness, elation, and a feeling of physical joy? A great litmus test is to also think of job roles that make you physically feel bad. Do you cringe merely thinking about certain projects in your job, or do you look forward to those tasks? Now write down what experiences in the past have made you feel constricted or unhappy. Is your behavioral life, your public persona, at odds with the values, beliefs, desires, passions, and visions that define your authentic self? Wow—that's a lot to think about but well worth the time.

This above all else: to thine own self be true.

SHAKESPEARE

Don't "Should" On Yourself

It's a rule of life that you get what you tolerate. Every day, through what you say and do, you teach others how to treat you. If you allow others to take you for granted or overstep your personal boundaries, you partner right along with them. You are also the biggest culprit when you allow guilt or expectations to make you cross your own boundary lines. Be clear about what you want and need, and forget what you "should" have to do with your life … and then be firm. Sticking to your wants is crucial to both your professional success and personal well-being. Live in a way that conveys that you know your worth.

- **Ask for what you want.** The truth is that no one else cares about your needs, preferences, and desires as much as you do. When you get clear about what you want and are brave enough to ask for it, you will spare yourself a lot of emotional headache and expand your capacity to accomplish more.

- **Don't limit yourself.** You are limited only by how much you limit yourself. We are all capable of achieving wonderful things, but we tend to limit our potential with our personal excuses: *I don't have time to do that. I don't have the energy to do this. I'm not ready.* Is there ever a right time? Sometimes "Just Doing It" is what it's all about.

- **Just say "no."** Saying "no" to others gives you the opportunity to say "yes" to yourself. It also gives you a chance to determine what your options are. As women, we tend to be people pleasers and quickly say "yes" for fear of not being liked. What we end up with is doing a lot of things we really don't want to do, and we set ourselves up for powerlessness. So say, "I'll get back to you." Offer your own suggestions. Say "no" to what you don't want so you can say "yes" to what you do.

- **Be direct.** Hints don't work and nobody can read your mind. Be specific about what you want and when you want it. Speak directly with confidence, in non-confrontational ways, and don't dilute your requests. Being direct and being aware is all about communicating well.

- **Ditch the guilt-driven martyr act.** Enough! It is not okay to feel guilty when you put your needs ahead of others (including the family pets)! The more you get caught in the trap of being all things to all people, the more you wind up feeling resentful and burnt out. Moving your own needs higher on the priority list is not selfish; it's smart! Your needs matter, too. Literally place yourself at the top of your to-do list and perhaps have your workout be, "That first frog you eat."

Complaining doesn't solve anything and whining about unmet needs won't fulfill them. Ditch the guilt and ask for what you really want. If you don't ask, you'll never get!

The Secrets Of Happy Women

Ever wonder how some women who seem to live such blessed lives are sometimes the unhappiest and discontent women you know? Then there are others whose lives seem to carry an unfair burden of losses and challenges, yet they live life with joy in their hearts and a twinkle in their eyes? What do they know that we don't?

We found out, based on research and through interviews with our female clients, what makes women happy. Now we get to let you in on their secrets of what you need to know to glide through the ups and downs of life with supersized smiles!

- **Take personal responsibility for your life.** Everything in your life has been about the choices you have made. Some might have been better than others, but they created who you are and what your life looks like today. Once you accept this, not only do you have more peace about your past, but you also become a better decision maker and become empowered to take action toward a more empowered life.

- **Live a meaningful life.** Happiness comes from having a sense of purpose and belonging. It comes from the opportunity to engage in things for which you are passionate about and that personally give meaning to you internally—not externally.

- **Serve others.** Giving to others helps to take your mind off yourself. When you make a contribution to someone or something, you feel valuable, which in turn builds your personal outlook, confidence and sense of joy. This altruism allows you to use your strengths to make a difference.

- **Nurture optimism.** Happiness is something you choose. You don't have to be a naturally positive person to practice looking at life's challenges in the best light possible. There is always a lesson to be learned from even the most challenging of circumstances. Approach adversity in as useful and optimistic way as possible.

- **Know yourself.** Do you really even know what makes you happy? We tend to be clearer about what we don't like, but take time to recognize how it's the simple things in life that end up giving you the most joy.

- **Fake it!** If all else fails, fake it till you feel it. Research demonstrates how powerful putting a smile on your face can be. You can trick your body systems into believing all is well, which feeds back to a positive shift in your mental processing.

Happiness is a way of being, and it's accessible to all. So be proactive and go out and get your happiness ... it's all around and waiting for you!

Attutude Of Gratitude

Waking up EVERY morning with the attitude of gratitude takes practice but it can be done! Martin Seligman, the father of positive psychology, discovered that subjects who practiced gratitude were overall happier and even less depressed.

- **Start a gratitude journal.** We have all heard about this, and it's true that when you write down three things you are grateful for each day you foster the attitude of gratitude. Don't judge. Think of being grateful for even the bad things that happen. Instead of looking at the glass as half empty, always try to see it as half full.

- **Say thanks and mean it.** Really, do you ever go up to your boss and say, "Hey, thanks for hiring me," or "I appreciate the project you gave me and am excited to get started with it." Thanking someone from the heart sets you up in an appreciative mindset, has them appreciate you more, and fosters trust and more opportunities in the future!

- **Handwritten notes of thanks.** Handwritten notes of gratitude symbolize a lot. They mean you cared enough to buy nice stationary, grab a good pen, and even more so, you took the time to think about that person and hand write your thoughts. Martin Seligman takes this concept a step further in his book *Flourish*. He encourages us to write a hand written note and then deliver and read it aloud in person.

- **Create a Gratitude Box.** Grab a big box or buy a decorated storage bin and designate it as the "Gratitude Box." Your Gratitude Box can store mailing stamps, colored pens, ink pads & stamps, stickers, gifts tags, stationary, and birthday cards. You can use it on a regular basis to send thanks and connect to friends, family, and people who matter to you.

- **Play the game of gratefulness.** At your next meal or dinner party dare to go around the table and ask people what they are grateful for. Why hold that tradition just at Thanksgiving?

- **Be of Service.** Your ability to give always comes back ten-fold. Make a visit unexpectedly to someone who is in need. Just show up without any agenda. Ask "How can I help you?" or "What do you need?" Volunteer!

A grateful mind is a great mind
which eventually attracts to itself great things.

PLATO

Maintain Curiosity

Many geniuses have the trait of curiosity. Curiosity allows you to ask the question "why," which in turn provides answers to the unknown. Practicing curiosity makes your mind stronger and keeps you adventurous, playful, and young at heart.

- **Adopt a growth mindset.** Open up your mind to explore new things without judgment; do not conform to the same old ideas. How about trying a Zumba, yoga, or belly dance class instead of the same old treadmill? Encourage your employees and family to practice growth mindset by allowing them to teach you a few new skills.

- **Be a student.** Explore different educational experiences, from cultural events and local venues to online and adult education classes. Sign up for courses at your local community college or university. Become a member of the museum or local gardens and attend their classes. Why not learn a language? Sign up at The Berlitz School or an adult education language or literature class. Try Rosetta Stone's lessons on DVD or even pick up language CDs free at the library.

- **Be curious—ask questions.** Take the time to find out from others why they do what they do or believe in what they believe. This curious attitude exemplifies acceptance and recognition of possibilities. Curiosity takes you out of routine and fills your life with adventure. By far, curiosity is one of the key ingredients to remaining youthful.

- **Explore other cultures and worlds.** Plan a two-week trip to a destination you have always wanted to go to but feared about not knowing enough about the language or culture itself. English speakers are everywhere and part of travel is enjoying the unknown. Peruse legitimate online vacation rentals and rent a house in a country you would love to be in for more than a week. Barcelona,

Beijing, Bermuda ... Istanbul, Iceland, Italy ... Spain, Singapore, or Senegal! The possibilities are endless.

Curiosity allows you to meet uncertainty with a positive attitude. Curiosity keeps you young and in tune with what's going on.

"We keep moving forward, opening new doors, and doing new things, because we're curious and curiosity keeps leading us down new paths."

WALT DISNEY

Build Your Personal Power

Personal power is almost indefinable, but we all know when we feel it and sense it in people who carry themselves with that something extra that draws us towards them. Personal power exhibits two main concepts: taking responsibility and action in your life. You feel secure in who you are and you are clear about what you want. You don't need to be right all the time, or be the most popular, or even have great wealth to have personal power. It is nurtured from within and is so influential in helping you achieve what you want in life.

- **Grit is the way to go.** This just might be your strongest weapon in battling the challenges of life. It's motivation, courage, and perseverance wrapped up into one quality that demonstrates a dedication that is valued by others.

- **Don't play the blame game.** You are not a victim, but rather a strong, courageous woman with the power to overcome difficulties and reach your goals. Believe this and participate in creating your own destiny every day by being proactive and setting daily goals that are small, measurable, realistic and doable.

- **Develop your emotional intelligence.** Concepts like self-awareness, self-management, empathy, and motivation all combine to create a powerful force that benefits both your personal and professional interactions and relationships.

- **Always a role model.** Tap into your best self and make decisions and act as if you are a leader in every moment of your day. Develop key traits that are valuable for your personal journey such as adaptability, resilience, perseverance, optimism, and even humor to draw others towards you. As you live, you will be!

- **Grow your trust worthiness.** Become a good listener. Take the time to be in the moment and really connect with someone as you hear what they say. Be dependable and reliable. If you honor your words, others will too.

- **Expand your network.** Take advantage of all the extra support from the connections and relationships you have in your life. Let them bolster your confidence and reassure you that you can handle whatever challenges life throws out at you. Give without any expectations in return, be generous and know that the return of investment will come back ten-fold.

People with personal power radiate contagious energy. Develop yours and see how your life can transform!

THE POWER OF BALANCE

The best and safest thing is to keep a balance in your life, acknowledge the great powers around us and in us. If you can do that, and live that way, you are really a wise (wo)man.

EURIPIDES

Kate is a busy executive with long work days. Kate likes her job and she fits in early morning workouts, but feels like she is missing "fun" in her life. She knows that having more balance in her life will decrease her stress, help her to feel more in control of her schedule, and be more joyful, but she was struggling to make any lasting changes. We started by encouraging her to find some time to be with friends she enjoys spending time with. Kate designated Saturday mornings to connect with these friends over coffee, to hit some yard sales, and to simply spend quality time with others. Kate is *energized* from being with those who feed her sense of well-being. As a result she has a better sense of balance in her life. She says, "I feel more *effective* in leading a life that is fulfilling by making meaningful connections with friends a priority."

The Present of Presence

You may take pride in your ability to do multiple things at the same time in the name of efficiency and optimal productivity. But the reality is you are often less productive if you multi-task. Always worrying about what "could have, should have, and would have" leads to quick mental burn out, and there is no future in always thinking ahead or lamenting the past. Being mindful, or present, is all about keeping focus on what is going on in that moment of your day.

Living in the present can calm the mind and decrease stress and anxiety. Mindfulness in all its simplicity is just letting yourself relax enough to appreciate what is going on in the here and now. It doesn't have to be more complicated than that. Here are some simple ways to incorporate being more mindful into your busy days.

- **Shhh!** Make time in your life for silence. Whatever you want to call it—meditation, prayer, quiet time—make time to enjoy the sounds of peace. Close the door, sit quietly, and just enjoy no interruptions, no one needing anything—just you and your quiet self. Look and draw all that you see into your inner world in a calm and thoughtful manner.

- **Check-in.** Check-in with yourself throughout your day to assess how you're feeling. Are you hungry, tired, overwhelmed, stimulated, energized? You are able to make better decisions when you take the time to check into your own internal compass. Are you headed North in the right direction, are you heading South the direction you want to avoid. You will be surprised at how much calmer and in control you feel by just knowing you are on course.

- **Find the beauty in routine activities.** Bring awareness to the daily activities you usually perform on autopilot. For example, pay attention to the sights, sounds, smells, and tastes as you brush your teeth, take a shower, or eat breakfast. Enjoy the small pleasures hidden within the daily grind. You might find that these routine activities are more interesting than you thought and that beauty, wonderment, and awe are everywhere.

- **Stop and listen.** Stop and make a conscious effort not to just hear the sounds, but to also actively listen. Hear the words and feelings of others. Maintain eye contact, nod your head, and make a concerted effort to listen without thinking of how you will answer.

- **Use a reminder.** Choose a cue that occurs in your daily life to remind you to be more mindful. It could be saying thanks before you eat or posting a quote on your desk—the key is to let it be the reminder to shift your brain into mindful mode.

- **Practice your meditation muscles.** The ideal is to meditate first thing in the morning for 20 minutes—the reality is to practice it any chance you can sit quietly and close your eyes without falling asleep. Every attempt has some value.

Mindfulness is being in control without a need to take control. It's slowing down enough to just be in the present moment. It's permission to stop and smell the roses!

Take Back Your Time

There is only so much time in a day and you cannot take back time. Time runs its course whether you want it to or not. There are only three ways to spend time—on thoughts, conversations, or actions. Choose the ones that lead you to success and dump the rest.

- **Be brutal!** What do you really need and want to accomplish today? Do not waste time and energy on tasks that really aren't important to you. List only your top tasks to do each day and dump the rest. Also tackle the biggest problem of the day first thing and cross that off the list!

- **Where is your time going?** We all have the same 24 hours in our day. What are you spending yours on? Track your time for three weeks to see where you spend it. Are there tasks you can bundle, delegate or delete? Discover where is your time most productive and where is it not. Then take the time to change where you focus your time.

- **Pick a system and stick with it.** We all have day timers from the 80s and online tools from the 90s, and there are always the yellow sticky notes. Find which time management system works best for your tendencies and style, and don't look back. Trust your system!

- **Share the load.** Delegation is the name of the game. Look at your daily to-do list and determine what you can delegate to someone else or to technology. Empower others to take over responsibilities and trust them to do what they do best. Let online banking, database management, online calendars and time management systems save you time.

- **Put an end to your workday.** There is no start and stop to the workday anymore. Long gone are the eight-hour days because now we connect with work 24/7. It's up to you to communicate that you conclude your work day at a certain time. Enjoy a few hours of anything but work. Be European, take all your vacation time and use your weekends to experience and enjoy life to the fullest!

- **<u>Schedule yourself into your schedule.</u>** Let yourself onto your calendar. Yes, make an appointment with yourself. Take your calendar and schedule exercise time, creative time, and social time: include time for family and friends. Plan a long weekend, or make some time for a manicure, haircut, or just time away from the office. Physically scheduling these events into your calendar will have you be accountable to yourself.

Don't look at time management as developing new ways of being more productive. It's not just about trying to control your time, but rather, on how to prioritize and live according to what's truly important to you.

Tame The Monkey Mind

The word "Monkey Mind" comes from a Buddhist term meaning unsettled, indecisive, or confused. Like a monkey jumping from tree to tree, our mind jumps from thought to thought. We all experience this mindset when we have too much to do and become overwhelmed. Here are some ways to calm that frenetic mind.

- **Step away.** Remove yourself—physically—from the overwhelming place you are in, whether it is your office or place of work. Move to a different room. Go to a café. Go for a walk. Gain clarity by literally seeing the issues at hand from another vantage point!

- **Move it.** Get up from what you are doing, yawn, stretch, and then run in place for 30 seconds. Increase that dopamine in the brain so you are able to come back to your task focused and alert.

- **Let go of judgment.** Society, advertising, workaholism, and stereotypes of beauty are just some situations that create stress and judgment. Make a conscious effort not to judge people or events as good or bad. Emotions, experiences, actions, and thoughts are not all good nor are they all bad, right, or wrong. Judging is DIRECTLY affecting your level of happiness and clogging up your mind. So don't be critical; stop and let go of it.

- **Journal it.** Write down all your thoughts on paper to get them out of your head. Dump them out onto a piece of paper to free up mental space. Make a list. Once written out, sort your thoughts into categories to gain a clearer perspective on what needs to be prioritized and what needs to be thrown away. Whittle that list down to a few items of top priority.

- **Ignore the inner critic.** Get away from that inner critic that says, "You cannot do this" or "You are not good enough." Start to think of those as merely thoughts you can recognize and then get rid of. Recognize the inner critic statements, disown them, and then feel them float away. Focus on your strengths and your own talents.

THE 5 POWER HABITS

- **<u>5 Minute Meditation.</u>** Calm the mind through meditation, yoga, or martial arts. Or simply sit up straight in your chair. Start by telling each part of your body to relax. Visualize sand flowing though your body as you do this. Focus then on an object like counting your breath. If other thoughts arise, get back to your focus, which is just counting your breath.

"Be master of the mind rather than mastered by the mind"

ZEN PROVERB

Get Organized!

What do your environments say about you ... controlled or cluttered? As homes and closets get bigger, we buy more to fill them. The challenge is maintaining and keeping all these things in order. The more stuff we have, it seems the less time we have to keep it all organized.

Living in a cluttered and disorganized environment also makes your mind more cluttered. Give your senses a break and commit to living with less stuff and more intention. Buy only what you need, when you need it, and make sure you love it. Remember, the less stuff you have, the less you have to organize and the more productive and focused you can be!

- **Clear out the daily crap!** Excuse our language, but women tend to drive themselves crazy with being the most disorganized in the places they use the most. So let the gift wrap closet go and instead focus on finally clearing off your desk, purse, wallet, inbox, car, and that miscellaneous drawer in the kitchen!

- **Are you a hoarder?** You may not warrant being on TV, but most of the time you may not realize you're creating a collection of junk because it happens so gradually. Be very critical and careful about what you bring into your environments. Delay the purchase of an item. Only use cash to buy impulse items. Ask if the purchase serves a purpose today, if it's necessary or something you could do without.

- **Clutter clean out.** Pick a weekend and then just do it! Get rid of the following: useless tchotchkes, costume jewelry you don't wear, gifts that aren't your taste, books and CDs that are downloaded or that you won't utilize, anything from your childhood that really doesn't have significant meaning, random memorabilia, cards or notes that you will never read again, and anything that just isn't you. Head to the dump where there is no return.

- **Create happy homes.** As the saying goes, "a place for everything and everything in its place." By creating homes for everything that make sense to you and that are easy to access, you are on your way to eliminating the piles and stacks that seem to grow around you.

- **The power of now.** Stop procrastination and do it now, put it away now, or deal with it now! End your workday with five minutes of desk clean-up and organize it for the next day. It will minimize the amount of time you spend looking for things and thinking about what you need to get done.

- **Outsource.** Hire a cleaning service, utilize party planners and caterers, use dry cleaners to launder … outsource whatever you hate or avoid doing. Don't feel guilty and instead spend time on things that bring more value to your life.

Get rid of the old clutter and keep the new organized you. We promise you will be a much happier woman!

Simplify, Simplify, Simplify

Living simply doesn't mean you have to live an ascetic lifestyle with forced poverty and no luxuries or indulgences. Who wants to sign up for that? Rather, it boils down to being satisfied with what you need rather than what you think you want. It means taking only what you need. It means being free to do what you really love in life. Living contently so you don't need a lot of extra "stuff" to fill your life means living an authentic and successful life that you get to define.

- **Re-evaluate your life.** Take a step back and think about what is truly important to you. What do you really want to be doing, who do you want to spend your time with, and what do you want to accomplish with your work? Make a short list of four to five things for your life, four to five people to spend time with, and four to five things you want to accomplish with work.

- **Detox!** It's time to finally get rid of the excesses and negatives in your life. Detox from people who give you more grief than joy, from things that aren't good for your body, from the "shoulds" and distractions in your life, and from everything that stresses you out and that just doesn't belong in your ideal way of living.

- **Live with less.** Take on "consumption reduction." When you decrease your needs for goods and services, you increase savings which moves you closer toward financial independence.

- **Make more time for quality time.** Be very frugal with your time, choosing things that bring you the most joy and fulfillment. Pursue creative interests and experiences that further your own personal growth and well-being.

- **Slow it down.** Whatever you are doing, whether big, small, important or not, slow down and enjoy every task. Stop thinking about other things and be completely in the moment and centered on what you are doing. Eat slower, drive slower, enjoy cooking your meals, and be more mindful in all the moments of your day.

- **Increase your self-sufficiency.** Stop consuming and start producing! Get back to the land and grow as much of your food as you can. Or at a minimum, eat sustainably with most of your foods coming from locally-grown and raised, seasonal, and fresh sources.

- **Downsize your schedule.** Reduce the number of commitments to just the essential ones and leave space between tasks for transition times. Say "no" to whatever is not aligned with your goals and leave room for down time and more fun.

- **Set boundaries.** Time is something you can never get back in life. Make boundaries for technology, your energy, communications, and work time. Simplify your to-do list to just the essentials. This allows you to rush less and focus on what's important.

Get clear about what you want and what you love and simply enjoy living your life!

Stress-Free Living

Buzz, Beep, Ding—we're programmed to bolt at the sound of an alarm, but can it also awaken you to what really matters in your life? Imagine the church bells calling you to prayer, or the school bells calling you to learn. How do you choose to live your life? What do you spend your time on and is it really meaningful?

Take a look at the structure of your life and determine if how you choose to live is setting you up for a stressful existence. Maybe the alarms are calling out to make some changes and work toward a more enjoyable and lower stress way of living.

- **Stay away from the office drama.** Office politics rates at the top of stressors at work. Like most people, you probably just really want to do a good job and be valued for your work. So focus on what you can control and stay as far away as you can from the rest of it.

- **Create a stress-free weekend.** Rituals are a great way to share the household responsibilities for half the day and then play as a treat for the second half of the day. Dedicating concrete time for household chores will help reduce stress during the week, and everyone knows to schedule out the day as a priority. End the day with something special and fun as a pay-off!

- **Create rituals.** Formalize the positive habits in your life that make the most difference to your well-being. You are what you repeatedly do, so give those actions that enhance your daily life a structured piece of your day. From sitting with a cup of coffee, to reading the paper, to an end-of-the-day soak in the tub, these acts are one less thing to think about and one more added pleasure to your busy life.

- **Plan to be early.** Being late to commitments is one of the most stressful things in your day. Try to leave earlier for everything by getting ready earlier or by scheduling more time between events. Being late disrespects other's time and places your "must complete" tasks ahead of them. Things always tend to take longer than you expect and it really is much better to be earlier to events than running late.

- **<u>Failure leads to success.</u>** Focus on the success in failures. Learn the lessons. When you accept that you really don't have much control over what happens in life, you enjoy the journey rather than focusing on achieving the end result. We all make mistakes. If you look at mistakes as learning opportunities, you are headed toward improvement and success.

Although life will never be truly stress-free, listen for the bells that call out to say that the levels are getting too high. Make some changes to keep stress as something that challenges you and helps you grow, rather than leading you to poor health and unhappiness.

Live In Moderation

When it comes to moderation, a little bit of something is good, but a whole lot of it is not necessarily better and may even lead to more harm. Exercise is a perfect example of this. We all know the benefits of getting in our activity, but you can easily cross the line where you do more damage to your physical self and increase your risk for injuries by overdoing it.

Being extreme in anything you do usually gets you into trouble, and women tend to be excessive in a handful of areas that are worth paying attention to. It's easy to get caught up in your busy life and then feel the need to dive deeply into something that is going to give you some temporary relief. If you dive too deep, however, you can end up creating more issues to deal with, which creates more stress in your life and ends up affecting your health in a negative way. So take a look at the following categories and make sure you are being balanced and moderate where it really counts.

- **Budget.** It's every woman's responsibility to take control of her financial future for herself and the well-being of her family. No shopping trip is worth the self-confidence you achieve from having fiscal stability. Pay cash as often as possible and balance your budget!

- **Commitments.** Women are notorious for having the disease to please. You don't want to hurt anyone's feelings, so you may say "yes" when you really want to say "no." Protect your time and energy fiercely and only say "yes" when you really mean it.

- **Sleep.** That little extra you can get done if you stay up late is not worth the toll it takes the next day. Too little of something important is just as damaging as getting too much. Sleep feels good, it makes you look good, and your body needs it.

- **Calories.** Sure, you eat for nourishment, but more often than not, women eat for taste, pleasure, escape, stress relief, and sometimes just because it's right there in front of you! Of course, you also know that too much eating of anything takes you to places you don't want to be. Nutrient dense foods, despite their smaller portion sizes can add up in calories as well—imagine just one coconut rolled almond stuffed dried date is 160 calories. There is no way around it ... *calories in versus calories out.*

- **Alcohol.** One glass of wine is wonderful, so two or more should be heavenly, right? Well, not so much the next morning! The health benefits for women are in the first glass of red wine each day. Nothing good happens after that first glass!

When you live in moderation, you take things in a little bit at a time—enough time to enjoy and savor the experience. Slow down and be moderate in all the things that you do for a chance at the most successful kind of living.

Face Time

Social connections improve physical health and overall well-being. Connecting with family and friends is a key to happiness and longevity, and has even been proven to increase immune system function. People who connect with one another also have lower incidence of depression and anxiety.

- **Blast the past.** Write down the top ten most important people in your life and how long ago you last connected with each. How often do you wish you could talk to them? Go to your calendar and schedule in regular reminders to catch up with each person. And stay off e-mail—even if you end up just leaving a nice voice message, hearing a voice helps you stay better connected.

- **Make a date to meet.** Meet someone for coffee this weekend. Make a lunch date this week. Plan a dinner with friends within the next two weeks. Pick the restaurant and time, and get that invitation out! Even schedule a slew of restaurant reservations for four to six people ahead of time and then invite your guests. The more often you see another person, the more intelligent and attractive you tend to find that person.

- **Connect via social media.** Just writing a quick e-mail with an article attached saying "This made me think of you" keeps us connected. Facebook has been an incredible way for people to share photos, articles, and activities across the globe. LinkedIn keeps you connected to colleagues who know other colleagues, making work connections a breeze. Instagram, Pinterist, and Twitter, though quick glimpses of your life, keep friends and family up-to-date, and can even lead to excellent opportunities for the future.

- **Community connections.** Get involved at the community level by joining your Chamber of Commerce, your neighborhood Civic Association, or local and national charities. Volunteer at community centers one day a month or once a week. Youth groups & clubs, libraries, and schools are a great place to start and continue to make a real difference in someone's life.

- **Throw a pot-luck party.** No one needs an excuse to plan and throw a party. Make it less daunting by making it a pot-luck. Guests love to bring and show off their favorite recipes, and it makes for a much lighter load for the hosts. There are even apps that help with that.

- **Delete energy zappers.** Forget hanging out with people who drain you. List the people in your life that fuel you—whom you feel energized by after being with. Commit to do more with those people. Know who your support systems are.

- **Don't have it your way.** Relationships are all about give and take—not having it your way all the time and learning to compromise helps you enjoy others for who they are. Misunderstandings often happen because of a lack of communication. Take time to communicate your wishes and feelings. Take time to listen well. It's also helpful to agree to disagree in some cases. You can only change yourself, so make that work to your advantage.

Brene Brown, a research professor at the University of Houston studying social connection, claims that at the root of human desire is the need to belong and connect. That does not mean you need a million friends on Facebook. Studies show the sense of connection varies among individual and just having a few good friends is just as important.

No Hocus Pocus In Focus

Focus—stick to one task and do it well. Research shows that multi-tasking, or doing more than one thing at a time, decreases productivity. The following simple tips are designed to help you focus so you are smarter, more efficient, and ultimately perform your best.

- **Focus on three.** Create a list of the top three small goals you will tackle each day. Achieve these three goals every day no matter what. Eat that frog by doing the most challenging task first and feel your joy as you cross it off the list. The challenge here is to keep your list to just three goals.

- **Start single-tasking.** If you're on the phone, get off the computer. If you are talking to someone face-to-face, stop texting. If you are eating, get away from your desk and sit at a table. To be more productive, focus on one thing at a time.

- **Record distractions.** Write down your top five distractions and delete two of them. By tomorrow, think about how you can have all five deleted. One client reported, *"I stopped looking at my instant messages by silencing my phone, avoided being distracted by e-mails, by turning off the e-mail notification window, and went to the library to work to get away from distractions."*

- **Find your prime time.** Do your most challenging, focused, and creative work during your prime energy times. Circle the times that most apply to you.

    5-8am   8-11am   11am-2pm   2-5pm   5-8pm   8-10pm

- **Clock it!** Determine how productive you really are by using a timer. Set your alarm for an hour from now. Work for a full hour uninterrupted and then get up from your task. (You can stretch in between.) Do not answer the phone, check e-mails, get on social media, or get up to eat and drink during this sacred time.

- **Track it!** Track your time on your calendar. Everything you do, find out your most productive times of day. After three weeks of recording, delete unwanted tasks that are not on purpose or that you can delegate. Highlight those times that work and stick to the new routine.

- **<u>Check social media at meal times.</u>** Turn off social media while you work. That includes the pop-up reminder on your e-mail responder. Check and respond to social media only at meal times. Yes, three times a day—maybe a snack time, too!
- **<u>Productive meetings.</u>** Create an agenda for a meeting and stick to the key issues. At the end of the meeting summarize the key points and have participants take responsibilities with a deadline to get it done. Decline meetings that are unproductive.

"Lack of direction, not lack of time, is the problem. We all have twenty-four hour days."

ZIG ZIGLAR

The Balanced Leader

It's time to move from working harder and faster to working smarter and more effectively, with more energy and better balance. Today's fast-paced living requires that you have new leadership skills to navigate the rapidly changing global landscape. You need to be a change agent and visionary in order to survive today's pace of life. Balance is personal. Structured schedules and rigid role definitions need to be more fluid to accommodate for greater flexibility, flow, and energy. You need to identify what personally motivates you and brings you fulfillment in life, and then fill your plate with that.

- **Focus on the journey, not the outcome.** How you live day-to-day is more impactful than the end result. Remember, balance is not a destination, but rather a practice filled with strategies, tools, and principles that you practice on an on-going basis.

- **Put it in writing.** Be a master planner and be proactive in making your calendar reflect what you intend to do, be, and accomplish in your life. Prioritize and schedule balance into your life—everything from doctor appointments to vacation and nights out. Your calendar should be a reflection of the different dimensions of who you are and what is important to you.

- **Know thyself.** Leadership is highly powerful when it comes from a place of authenticity. When you understand your own personal strengths, weaknesses, values, and passions, you are able to connect with others more effectively and make better decisions in your life. Be true to yourself and take the time to check-in to make sure your life reflects what is meaningful to you.

- **Play President.** Imagine if you were the President of the United States or a big celebrity where every choice and action you make is not only being watched, but also imitated by others. Would being healthy, having meaningful relationships, or supporting social causes be important components of your life? Act as if you are an important role model and you might find yourself leading a more balanced life.

- **Delegate, dump, or do.** Drop the activities that zap your time and energy. Stay away from the colleague who is constantly venting and gossiping to you. Take stock of the activities that don't enhance your career or personal life and minimize your time spent on them. Be an effective and balanced leader by streamlining your life.

- **Get real.** One of the biggest challenges for women is that we think we can do more than we really have the time and energy for. We end up setting high expectations that are difficult to follow-through on. Be realistic with what you really can accomplish in your daily 24 hours and be a leader who is able to match what you say you can do to what you are actually able to do.

- **Create supportive environments.** Make it easier for you to maintain balance in your life by making your environments at work and home more supportive. Whether it's healthier foods served at meetings or a kitchen stocked with fresh produce when you come home, you will be better able to achieve what is important to you if you have convenience and support built in to your life.

Leaders who put their personal goals first are more productive and have more energy. They are living with balance internally and externally.

THE POWER OF REJUVENATION

> *We must always change, renew, rejuvenate ourselves otherwise we harden.*
>
> JOHANN WOLFGANG VON GOETHE

Lee is a busy working mother with a demanding job that requires her to be connected to some form of technology at all times. Not only does she constantly check her phone and e-mails once she is at home, but it means that she is constantly distracted and unable to enjoy quality family time with her ten-year-old son and husband. One evening at the dinner table, she noticed that no one was talking to each other and all three of them were doing something with their phones while they were eating. This had become a habit at their home without anyone even realizing it! Lee was horrified that she was setting a bad example for her son and she decided to make technology forbidden for all three of them at the dinner table and after 9:00 p.m. when they could all spend 30 minutes playing a game together, watching comedy shows, and doing whatever they felt like in the moment. Very quickly, Lee looked forward to her evenings and felt *empowered* by setting a good example to her son. She also felt more *effective* when she was working. As she says, "Making room to clear my mind inspires me to rejuvenate, to enhance my wellbeing, and to increase my productivity."

Sleep Is Not A Luxury

You know it's good for you, you enjoy it, and you know you don't function as well when you don't get enough. Why, then, are we such a sleep-deprived society? Good quality sleep is so vitally important to your health, productivity, and mood, yet you may still convince yourself that you can get by on fewer hours to work or play harder. Sleep is not optional. A sleeping brain is actively re-regulating all of the body's critical systems, including the immune system, mental and memory consolidation, and muscle and cellular repair. It's also the cheapest and most effective beauty treatment around!

The following are ways to create some supportive habits to get you on your way to a more restful, restorative, and rejuvenating sleep—along with just more of it!

- **Personalize your sleep schedule.** Determine how many hours your body personally needs by letting yourself naturally wake up and see what number consistently comes up. Then pick a bedtime schedule and stick with it. For hard data try monitoring your sleep with nighttime gadgets, which are now available in wristbands and arm bands to track your most restful and awake times during the night. See if a pattern emerges from those nights you do the best.

- **The power of napping.** Napping doesn't just feel good in the moment; it also recharges your body and your brain with health-promoting benefits. Twenty to forty-five minutes is all you need to restore your mood and energy while decreasing your stress levels.

- **Enhance your bedtime experience.** Sounds racy, but what we're talking about is setting yourself up for an enjoyable sleep experience. Whether it's ways to decrease your emotional and physical stimulants or finding ways to create a cozy ambiance, make your bedtime experience more enjoyable.

- **Shut it down.** Yes, that means turning off every screen—TV, phones, computers, portable technology—anything with an off switch. Research is clear that electronic media right before going to sleep interferes with both the quality and quantity of sleep.

- **<u>Don't drink large amounts of fluids before bedtime.</u>** One of the most disruptive things to quality sleep is having to wake up to use the bathroom in the middle of the night. So take care of business before sleeping and avoid liquids before bedtime. Talking about drinks ... alcohol consumption can also interfere with sleep. Exercise can help with sleep if done at least two hours before bedtime.

Sleep on this—getting a good night's sleep (7-9 hours) is one of the most important things you can do for your overall health and well-being. Adequate sleep gives your body time to recover from the day's stresses, decreases depression, and helps you to stay sharp and focused throughout your day.

It's Playtime!

Who knew that pursuing your favorite amusements could have so many physiological and psychological benefits that can bolster your well-being? Research shows us that taking time out in your day for some fun can actually improve your concentration, boost problem-solving abilities, and enhance creativity.

What gets in the way of taking these breaks and goofing off is our own mistaken beliefs that idleness and play are indulgences and distractions from what we really "should" be doing. But these apparently low-productivity pursuits can actually move us toward being more effective thinkers, productive workers, and healthier, happier, and more resilient people. So take a break when you feel your energy or mood plummet and play!

- **Be spontaneous.** You used to say "yes" to impromptu lunch dates or get-away weekend trips. While you may now prefer planning to surprises, some amount of spontaneity is important to add spice to your routine and stimulate your brain.

- **Roam free.** When is the last time you let yourself physically wander, along with allowing your mind to roam free in its thoughts? Both are valuable for self-renewal and to maintain an edge to your physical and mental abilities.

- **Sign up for some fun.** Add imagination and creativity into your life by signing up for a class or activity. Whether it's painting, playing music, pottery, or learning another language, you will be expanding yourself into new territories.

- **Daydream.** Stare out the window and give your conscious mind a break from having to constantly focus on tasks. This is one of the best ways to invite insights, ideas, and new solutions into your workday.

- **Take a 20-minute timeout.** Why is it that we often come up with our best ideas when we're in the shower or cooking? It's because we're finally relaxed and that's when our best thinking happens as our brain is free to do whatever it likes, including developing spontaneous insight. Build in time for 20 minutes of a mind break after every 90-120 minutes of work.

- **Goof off!** Share laughs with your co-workers, show your weekend pictures to others, and even re-hash last night's TV episodes at the water cooler. It all counts toward balancing your sense of eternal responsibilities and things you have to do.

- **Plan to escape.** Plan an hour away from the office with your colleagues. Escape to a museum, restaurant, or lunch time concert. Come back refreshed and inspired to end your day on a high note.

Pursuing random moments of "unproductive" time might be a whole lot more productive than you think. There is a lot of value in having some fun!

Get Away/Retreats

Ever notice that when you come back from vacation, a retreat, or a day away you can see the world with a brand new outlook? That's because getting away from routines is a way to refresh and see things from another perspective.

- **Experiences pay back.** Spend your hard earned money on experiences such as trips and special evenings out rather than on possessions or acquired things. Experiences can be banked in memory and grow richer over time.

- **Create a STAYCATION!** Think of where you live like a tourist would. Search out museums, fun parks, sports events, and cultural activities that are around you within 20 miles. Visit them as an out-of-towner would with food stops in between at favorite local beats. Take the time now to research online "fun guides" in your area and schedule two events in your calendar for the next month.

- **Plan mini adventures.** There is nothing like the thrill of getting away from the same old, same old. Get out of the monotony of every day and plan a picnic or a TV movie night. Pump up those old bike tires and go for a ride, head to the skating or roller rink for a night out or plunge into a fresh cool lake or ocean.

- **Weekend get-a-way.** How about a trip to Miami with three of your best friends? Stay in a top notch hotel off season and sip mojitos by the beach! Plan ahead for a romantic escape with your significant other. You do not have to go far to escape your routines and familiar environment. Search for package deals online or take advantage of quick cheap flights and hotels online.

- **Read to escape.** Escape the afternoon by getting Leisure and Travel magazines from the library. Note places you would like to visit in the future. Read travel books like Fodor's, Frommer's, or The Lonely Planet and start to make your dreams a reality.

- **Retreats.** Retreats are everywhere and provide great ways to get a hobby in while in the R & R mode. Do research on retreats about knitting, quilting, kayaking, cooking, and sports, as well as workshops from yoga to women's wellness. Get as far away from work as you can, meaning no workshops that are work related.

Vacation time is an opportunity to regroup and come up with new ideas. It is a time to unwind and de-stress, which helps you to be even more productive when you return to work. Breathe, recharge, and spend uninterrupted quality time with those you love. Book your vacation today.

"When all else fails, take a vacation!"

BETTY WILLIAMS

Get Unplugged

During the week, we are checking e-mails, social media, phone messages, and texts every moment we have. And what do we do during our downtime? TV, movies, online shopping, tablet reading, and maybe even video games. We are attached to some kind of screen for most of our waking hours! While technology has many worthwhile purposes, it demands a high price from us. Research shows that our increasing media dependency is crippling our attention spans, hurting our relationships, and generating a false expectation that we should be able to be contacted at every moment.

Break free and try one of these strategies. Prove to yourself that you are capable of surviving without being connected ... even if only for a few hours!

- **<u>Go off-grid for a few hours each day.</u>** Living without devices for a whole day is difficult. Start with a few structured hours in your day where it makes sense. Let others know not to try to reach you during this time and let yourself "switch-off" completely. You might be surprised at how relaxed you feel if you are able to drop the worry or guilt of not being connected.

- **<u>Make your bedroom and kitchen technology-free zones.</u>** The original intent for these rooms in our homes was not to do work, yet we have integrated some form of digital connection to two of life's greatest pleasures—eating and intimacy. We check e-mails before we go to sleep and we tend to have the TV on in our kitchens or dining spaces as a form of efficiency. Keep these two areas of your home sacred and enjoy them for what they were intended to be used for.

- **<u>Make it a family affair.</u>** Get your family on board and pick activities to do all together, but with no technology allowed! This will enable spouses, parents, and kids to build stronger bonds and communicate more personally.

- **Techno centerpiece.** When eating out, even with co-workers, have everyone put their phones in the center of the table ... on off-mode. It's a sight to behold when six phones are piled up as a pretty table centerpiece.

- **Go old school.** Put the gadgets down, away, or even get rid of them for good. We get excited anytime a new tech product comes out, but what we end up feeling is overwhelmed with adding on another app or upgrade we need to deal with. Instead, break out with a real book or paper for a letter and see how much more enjoyable the experience can be. All things new are not necessarily good!

Pull the plug at some point in your day and in some form. Take back the pleasure in looking at the world instead of a screen. Time to e-Tox!

Energy Boosters

Need energy? If you want it fast, grab a tall glass of cold water, get outside for some fresh air, and hit those stairs for a quick boost in your metabolism. But if you're reaching for your 4th cup of coffee and it's only 10:00 in the morning, you might want to consider filling your days with some healthy and natural ways to give you a much needed boost that will not only have an immediate effect, but will result in longer-lasting energy to help you power through your day.

- **Music.** Go ahead and get your groove on while you work! Listening to music invigorates the body by activating several areas of the brain at once. It also gives you an extra perk by increasing oxygen flow to your heart.

- **Take a breath … or two.** When you yawn and feel sleepy and sluggish, it's a signal that your body is trying to increase its oxygen intake. Take a few minutes to sit up tall and inhale deeply through your nose; hold it for three seconds before exhaling through your mouth. Repeat the cycle three to five times and feel recharged.

- **Energize your space.** Our work and living spaces can have a major impact on our energy levels. Light, color, noise, and smells all have the power to either energize or exhaust you. Notice what you personally respond to. Maybe all it takes is that citrus-scented hand lotion to give you a little pep in your day.

- **Go ahead and take that cat nap.** Aside from food, one of your body's main sources of energy is rest. Yet most people come into work every day completely sleep deprived and feeling weary, irritable, and unable to concentrate. Even just putting your head down on your desk and closing your eyes can give you enough of a break to return to your tasks with more pep.

- **Take on something new.** Avoid filling your day with the same schedule and with the same tasks. Research shows us that new experiences tend to give us a rush. When we do something new, the brain's reward chemical, dopamine, is released and we feel better about ourselves and energized from the experience.

- **Bring on the sunshine.** The neurotransmitters in your brain respond well to sun-bathed light and leave you feeling refreshed and stimulated. Sunlight also increases the body's production of serotonin, which lifts your mood and increases energy. So grab the desk near the window and head outside for "sun breaks." Use a sun lamp to lighten your mood if you live in northern climates for light therapy during those dark winter months.

Get energized, have quicker reaction times, feel better, and get more out of your day!

Laugh, Giggle, Smile ☺

Successful living should always include humor. A good belly laugh has been described as "internal jogging" for its health benefits and stress relief. And a good sense of humor has always been an enormous asset to your outlook on life and to your social life, as everyone enjoys being around funny people. Laughter improves many aspects of your immune system, boosts your energy, diminishes pain, and protects you from the damaging effects of stress. And the good feeling that you get when you laugh remains with you even after the laughter subsides.

- **Say cheese!** Smiling is the beginning of laughter. It has the incredible power of lifting others and our own moods in an instance. Make smiling your default response to others and see what a difference it can make to them and yourself.

- **Know where you can get a quick hit.** Keep some laughter on stand-by for those days when you really need it. Whether it's your favorite radio host driving into work or the late night shows that find a way to poke fun at the most mundane news of the day, use it as a distraction instead of hitting the nearest bakery!

- **Get a pet.** Nothing can bring a smile to your face than the unconditional love of pets. The simple joy of playing with your furry friends is a great way to bring more laughter and fun into your life.

- **Seek out playful people.** Spend as much time as you can with people who laugh easily—both at themselves and at life's absurdities. Their playful point of view and laughter are contagious and their perspective will help get you through tough times. So share the fun!

- **Don't take yourself so seriously.** Laugh at yourself. Share your embarrassing moments. Most events in life don't need to be taken so seriously. Find the humor and choose to see the lighter side of life.

- **Make time for fun activities.** Your ability to laugh, play, and have fun with others not only makes life more enjoyable, but also makes you more creative, helps you to connect with others, and renews your spirit and outlook. So hit the playground with the kids, go bowling with your co-workers, check out the laughing yoga class at the gym, catch the latest comedy club show for date night, and plan for game-night or karaoke with your friends.

The bottom line is that laughter feels good, it's cheap, always available, makes you look and feel younger, and you'll always have someone willing to share in the fun with you!

Read This

When was the last time you spent an afternoon lounging with Heathcliff? When life wears you down, there is nothing like a great story to take you away from the stresses of life and transport you to wonderful places and interesting story lines. Reading forces you to linger in your imagination and not on your task lists. Reading can also inspire and motivate you to go out and explore the places you are reading about or try something new that you were exposed to in the story.

Apart from the joy of sitting in one place and getting lost in a story, research shows that reading actually helps you to feel less isolated and more aware and attuned to others. You are better able to understand the human character and decipher the emotions and the perspectives of others.

- **Be inspired…for free!** When was the last time you walked into a library and not wished you spent more time reading? The books seem to call out to you and inspire you to learn and do more in your life. Public libraries also make it easy with free downloadable books as well as websites like www.gutenberg.org.

- **Join a book club.** But make sure you actually read the books! The fun is not only in the wine, chit-chat, and social time. You'll enjoy reading books that you might have never picked out on your own. Maybe you can even start a reading club at work.

- **Subscribe your reading.** Short, sweet, and visual. Reading doesn't mean only books. Order a subscription to a magazine, journal, or newspaper for short and ever-changing updates on exactly what you are interested in.

- **Listen to your words.** If you spend a lot of time commuting, take advantage of audio books. This is a personal favorite of ours that helps us get through the books we want to read while burning up the miles whether in the car or on foot.

- **Keep your reading near and dear.** Keep your reading materials easily accessible in all of your environments because you never know when you might be able to fill-in free moments and dead time. Read on the bus, train, while waiting to board a plane, or while you are waiting for an appointment.

Pick up a book and take a break from your life. Not only will you expand your knowledge, but you'll also enjoy a few moments of slowing down and diving into something much more interesting than your day planner!

Get Outside

No matter how urban you are, there is an ancient part of you that craves trees and grass, fresh air and sunshine. Nature is where your earliest ancestors derived their food and shelter, and thus there is a deep rooted sense of comfort when you spend time in the outdoors. For many it is the most restorative experience on the Earth. There is no better way to relax, recharge, and reconnect to your spirit than when you unplug your gadgets and get some R & R in nature.

Break free from being an indoor zombie with your dulled senses, depressed spirits, and lack of well-being. It's as simple as opening your door and stepping outside!

- **Here comes the sun.** How do you slip in a little bit of sun without heading to Hawaii? Head out for mini-walks in the morning or during your lunch break and eat outdoors whenever the weather permits. A little sunshine in moderation will help your body create vitamin D to support your bones and also gives you a little mental boost of happiness.

- **Keep it simple.** Getting outdoors doesn't mean climbing Mt. Everest. Even star-gazing or a ten-minute walk in the neighborhood or local park will calm your mind and help reconnect you with the bigger picture of life.

- **Kick off those heels!** When was the last time you ran around outside in the grass, sand, or dirt in your bare feet? Remember the feeling of the earth between your toes and how refreshing it is to feel carefree. Let yourself physically connect with the Earth and energize your spirit and your body.

- **Stimulate your senses.** Head to places that really speak to your sense of smell, sight, touch, and hearing. Fill your lungs with clean and fresh air instead of the re-circulated toxic air we are used to indoors. Listen to the peaceful sounds of nature and visually let your mind take in all of the beauty that surrounds you.

- **Stay in the big picture.** Choose outdoor places that really speak to you and help keep perspective in your life. What reminds you of happy childhood memories or creates a sense of healing within yourself? Head there and let the small worries and minutiae of the world slip away, as they can't compare to the timelessness of the trees and streams that have withstood the challenges of time. Be inspired by their resilience and let them remind you of your ability to get through tough times.

Get out of your homes and offices and head out of town to the beach, woods, or wherever the fresh air, sunshine, stars, and nature call to you!

Small Fixes For Big Results

Fast ... you need a quick fix for your lousy, long, stressful, tiring day and you need it now! The chocolate is calling your name, along with a glass—no, a bottle—of wine and whatever else that's lying around. Instead of heading down that rabbit hole again, keep this list handy and pick the actions that are the most realistic and fun and go ... now!

We all have those days—usually more often than we would like to admit. Unfortunately, your busy and fast-paced lifestyle sets you up for tiring days filled with things that don't always go the way you intended. This time, aim for the calorie-free joys in life and come out the other end of your challenging day truly feeling better.

- Take a bath with scented oils and candles
- Try a new recipe
- Watch a chick flick
- Grab a dog or friend for a long walk
- Clean and organize
- Spend time in a bookstore
- Go window-shopping
- Go to bed early
- Explore interesting classes or lectures
- Do a crossword puzzle
- Buy fresh flowers
- Flip through a magazine
- Catch up with an old friend
- Have a cup of tea
- Listen to great music
- Give yourself a facial

- Go to a museum
- Soak your feet
- Get to water—a beach, lake, river, stream, etc.
- Take a nap
- Get lost in a good book
- Get a mani/pedi
- Sing, shout, let it all out
- Walk to a park
- Sit in a café/people watch
- Go to a place of worship
- Light a scented candle
- Get a complimentary makeup makeover
- Go to a farmer's market
- Plan a party
- Find some sunshine
- Schedule a massage
- Plan a mini-vacation
- Write in a journal
- Plant a windowsill herb garden for cooking
- Get your hair styled
- Stretch or do yoga twists

Choosing a quick fix from this list will help get you to calm quickly and with a lot more lasting power than that pint of ice cream!

Make A Style Statement

The minute you walk into a room, people size up their impression of you. They watch how you walk, how you carry yourself, and as trivial as it seems, they notice what you are wearing. Have fun with developing a style that you are comfortable with and that makes an appropriate statement about who you are and the image you want to project.

Here are some tips to help you define your signature style. Your overall presence will speak volumes before you ever say a word!

- **What is your look?** Decide what statement you want your external appearance to make about you and your work. Do you want to project sophistication? Are you a trendsetter? Do you have an artistic flair?

- **Frazzled is not an option.** Casual does not mean sloppy. A rushed, disheveled look is never a good thing. Your attitude is influenced by your appearance, so put in the effort and take advantage of looking clean and fresh in your own way.

- **Streamline the process.** Keep things simple. We're not intending to add on to your to-do's, but rather once you create a "look" that works for you, it should make your shopping easier. You know your style and what works for you, so stick with it and ignore everything else. Pinterest is a fun platform to get ideas for getting inspired to hone in on your personal style.

- **Get help if you need it.** Whether it's personal shoppers or dragging your best friend with you when you shop, don't tackle it on your own if it feels overwhelming. Remember, this is supposed to make your life easier. Honest feedback from a trusted source can save you time and money.

- **Embrace your femininity.** Ditch the power suits—the goal is not to dress like a man! You have much more flexibility in today's world, so break out with the bright colors, frills, and bits of bling. Just keep it tasteful and respectful and stay true to you.

- **Have fun with it!** Let yourself be creative. Play around with different accessories. Explore different fabrics, colors, and styles that make you feel the most comfortable and confident. Don't be afraid to let your signature style show.

Clothing can be an expression of who you are. When you develop your own style, everyone sees you that way and you now have your own brand. That's great advertising!

THE POWER OF MOVE

> *My grandmother started walking five miles a day when she was 60. She's 97 now, and we don't know where the heck she is.*
>
> ELLEN DEGENERES

If not sitting at her desk, in the car, or in meetings, Samia finds herself sitting in planes for extended periods of time. In fact, she spends the majority of her waking hours on her bum! We worked with Samia to figure out how she might be able to fit in some fitness into her work day. We came up with making each daily meeting with her division managers at the end of the day a moving meeting. They hit the walking path by their office to get updates and strategize—all while getting a boost in their metabolism and increasing their productivity and *effectiveness* when back at work. This simple strategy has allowed her to get out into fresh air, burn some calories, meet face-to-face, and return *energized* and invigorated. "Exercising regularly boosts my mood and keeps me strong and focused, not to mention looking my best" says Samia.

Make Moving Fun

By now, you know all the good reasons for being active—you lose weight, get in shape, feel better about yourself, gain strength and stamina, increase your energy level, and increase your confidence. You also likely know what you should be doing—stretching, toning, and cardio for 20-30 minutes every day. What you really want to know, and what makes the biggest difference, is how to make exercise more fun!

- **Grab a gadget.** No matter what gadget or gizmo you prefer, tracking your movement in an objective manner has health benefits. Pedometers are our favorite for their ease and motivation to make us take extra steps throughout our day. The value of fitness gadgets are that they make pushing yourself feel more like a game. You can measure your success over time in miles, calories burned, and even through your heart rate. All of a sudden, walking a little extra doesn't seem so bad.

- **It's a dance party!** Any time there is upbeat music playing, your body naturally wants to move to the rhythm, so take advantage and pump up your workouts by moving to the beat! Whether you play music in your home and dance around the house or you use music to quicken the pace of your workouts, you will be sure to increase the fun factor of moving your body.

- **More about dancing.** Some new programs are combining dance and exercise, from Jazzercize and Zumba to Ballet Bar and Hip Hop. These classes are a great way to release stress, make some friends, enjoy, and get fit.

- **Sexercising.** Besides the pleasure factor, having sex is good for you mentally and physically, and it can help you live longer. While sex may not be the same as a boot camp class, your body is still getting some form of a muscular workout and burning calories. So let yourself get in the mood!

- **Jump in the pool.** Remember your childhood when nothing was more fun than swimming in a pool or jumping in a lake? Dive back in the water for some old school fun from laps, playtime with the kids, or even trying out a water aerobics class. Water provides natural resistance to help tone without the wear and tear on muscles.

- **Try something new.** Novelty is the best way to get out of a fitness slump and rev up your motivation. There are so many options out there—from various boot camps to paddle board yoga—that you are bound to find something that speaks to you.

Fun makes the difference between fitting exercising into your busy schedule or not. It also makes waking up at 5:30am in the middle of winter more of a reality. So try something new, grab a gadget, and get moving toward a good time! What's the point of being healthy if you're not having fun!

Mind-Body Activities

One of the best ways to enhance well-being is to integrate mind-body practices into your fitness routine. Their essence is simply based on using your thoughts and breath to influence your body's physical responses. Their healing abilities help to decrease stress, strengthen immune systems, minimize chronic pain, and enhance restorative sleep.

The following are by no way a comprehensive list of all of the fitness experiences available that develop the mind-body connection, but they are amongst some of the most popular and accessible throughout the world. Experience them all and decide which ones you naturally feel the deepest connection to and then integrate them into your fitness routine.

- **Keep it simple.** Engaging in a mind-body experience doesn't have to involve signing up for a fitness class that you can't pronounce. A simple 20-minute daily stroll can clear your mind, give you perspective, and ease stresses from your day. The key is to be engaged and mindful while you are also moving your body.

- **Breathe.** Meditation and relaxation use the power of your mind to focus on breathing, resulting in your body relaxing and your mind achieving calm.

- **Experience the Asian practices.** Whether it's Tai Chi or Qigong, these traditional Chinese energy practices are based on spiritual, martial, and health exercises. The harmonious movements are especially effective for developing balance, focus, coordination, and graceful, centered movement.

- **Yoga.** Yoga is an ancient discipline that connects the mind, body, and spirit through poses, concentration, and meditation. Although there are various modified versions today, yoga is designed to develop mental and physical health, inner harmony, and a communion between you and the universe.

- **Practice intuitive training.** Learn to listen to your body's cues and subtle changes in mood, coordination, balance, and heart-rate then adjust your activity accordingly. Getting intuitive helps you end up with a mind-body workout that develops a sharper kinesthetic sense, which helps avoid needless injuries and accelerates desired outcomes. You are able to focus on the process and not just on the end result.

- **Pilates.** These exercises emphasize breathing, form, and posture with the purpose of increasing flexibility, strength, and mobility, along with developing the torso. Pilates is excellent for anyone who suffers from lower back pain and a weaker central core.

Mind-body exercises not only improve flexibility, strength, posture, and balance, but also your coordination, stress levels, ability to focus, and inner well-being. Take advantage and peace out!

Stand Up Straight

Would you like to add an inch or so to your height...without having to wear high heels? All it takes is sucking in your gut, pulling your shoulders back, pushing your chest out, and looking straight ahead. *Voila*—you are taller, more poised, and confident!

Why do so many women walk around hunched and shrinking? Sure, gravity starts to take its toll as we age, and we are sitting hunched over our computers much more, but nothing makes us look as youthful and full of confidence than standing, sitting, and walking with good posture. It can also help us prevent common health problems such as back and neck pain, headaches, and fatigue, and avoid some of the effects of aging, like pressure on the spine and digestive issues. So take breaks throughout your day to stretch out and realign your body, and no more leaning back into bad posture!

- **Sit on it.** Work on your posture even while you're working all day long. Sit on a stability ball at your desk and force your back to have to strengthen its muscles to keep your body in proper alignment. There are even stability ball chairs with rollers and other ergonomically correct chairs, so you can look professional while strengthening your torso. The key is to be mindful of your posture.

- **Ditch the big bag.** How many of you can survive for a week with what you carry in your purse? The amount of extra food, papers, organizers, accessories, reading materials, glasses, and electronic gadgets we carry around with us is crazy! You will survive without receipts from last year in your wallet, so go small with only the essentials and save your right shoulder from being perpetually bogged down.

- **Work your core.** Whether it's through yoga, Pilates, or basic abdominal crunches, strengthening your core muscles is the best way to support good posture.

- **Sleep well.** How you sleep can have an effect on your waking posture. Using a firmer mattress and sleeping on your back will help to maintain proper back support. If you like sleeping on your side, use a small, flat pillow between your knees to keep your spine straight and aligned.

- **<u>Make driving work for you.</u>** Considering how much time we spend in our cars, take advantage of all of the seat adjustments in your car and use your head-rest to support sitting with good posture. Keep your upper back and shoulders flat against the seat. Remember, this is important for the car's safety systems to function properly.

Your mom was right when she used to remind you to "sit up straight" at the dinner table. Even though you may not have listened back then, it's never too late to start practicing.

Be Strong

When it comes to fitness, time always seems to be the limiting factor, and the first thing to go is any kind of strength training. You don't want to bulk up and you need to burn as many calories as you can to compensate for overindulging. This type of rationalization is not only false, but is really counterproductive to the overall goal of being lean and fit.

Strength or resistance training increases your muscle tissues, which happens to actually be smaller and leaner in dimension than the equivalent amount of body fat in weight, which has a softer and flabbier appearance. Your body also has to work harder to pump blood and nutrients to maintain the lean tissue, resulting in a higher overall metabolism compared to the amount of effort (calorie burn) it has to do to support your fat tissue.

Don't worry, you won't get huge. Women have lower levels of testosterone, which makes it difficult to be able to develop huge amounts of muscle mass. The goal is to shift our body fat percentage so you build more lean tissue as you decrease your body fat, resulting in less softness and flab and more of a strong and toned body.

- **Mix in your cardio.** Get your workout done in record time! Interval training involves high-intensity cardio activity in short bouts followed by longer bouts of strength training to maximize your calorie-burning capacity while still toning. Some exercise classes and videos are great ways to find out about these combos.

- **Get toned in the water.** The consistent resistant forces of being under water engages your muscle fibers through a large range of motion. You are able to firm from many different angles all with minimal risk of injuries.

- **Work your whole body.** Don't just focus on the small muscles like the biceps and inner thighs individually; work more muscles through a motion that involves both the small and large muscles. For example, an exercise that makes you pull something will work the muscles in your back, arms, and chest.

- **Use your body as natural resistance.** If you don't have easy access to weights or resistance machines, use your own body weight to do push-ups, squats, or other simple exercises that can be done anytime and anyplace.

- **Decrease aging!** Resistance training isn't just good for your muscles; it helps decrease aging by keeping your bones strong and your hormone levels more stable.

Don't be scared off by strength training. Being strong doesn't mean getting huge and "ripped". We're talking about the firm, toned, tight, lean, long, sculpted, and sexy version of resistance training. Sounds good, doesn't it?

Fitting Fitness In

Finding time in a busy schedule to exercise can be challenging. Including activity into your day is vitally important to your health, well-being, and your energy levels. The key is to make fitness convenient and flexible, and to be prepared to be creative in order to build movement into your schedule. Even Superman had to wear his uniform under his clothes in order to be ready to go at a moment's notice. Remember, the goal isn't to have perfect exercise routines, but rather to integrate as much movement into your day whenever and wherever you can. The following are some things you can do to fit movement into even the busiest of schedules:

- **Workout your commute.** Make running, biking, and walking to work both your workout and your form of transportation. Even getting off your bus or train a few stops earlier will build in some fitness and allow time for transition between both places.

- **Short bouts is where it's at.** We all have 10 minutes here and there. Fill the gaps in your schedule with ten-minute short bouts of moving in order to give yourself a little metabolism boost. Whether it's walking up and down the stairwell at work or walking around the block at home, every little bit counts toward making you a healthier person and feeling good about yourself.

- **Make room for fitness.** Set up a treadmill or stationary bike in front of the television in order to add some sweat to your TV time. If you find yourself sitting at your desk eight hours a day, why not look into a treadmill desk and treadmill.

- **Reinvent playtime.** Play games with your kids—shoot hoops, toss a ball, jump on a trampoline. Make date night something active and hit the outdoors by hiking or biking, bowling, or playing tennis with friends instead of hitting happy hour. You'll build in more smiles while burning more calories.

- **Walk and talk.** Take your meetings outdoors. Whenever you have a one-on-one meeting with someone amenable to it, discuss while you are walking outdoors. The fresh air and movement may even encourage creativity and problem-solving.

- **Wake up to fitness.** Getting your workout in first thing in the morning will get you energized and feeling empowered for the rest of the day. As the day progresses, it often gets busier, so for most people the morning is an optimal time for exercise.

- **Exercise while traveling.** Plan for activity on the go by bringing the appropriate clothing and shoes and create time into your travel schedule for exercise. Do some research before you go. Also, take advantage of hotel gyms and outdoor walk/runs in different cities.

Make your workouts work for you and make fitness a way of life. Remember, all physical activity, not just formal workouts, add up to a healthier you.

Metabolism Boosters

Your metabolism is a complex network of hormones and enzymes that not only convert food into fuel, but also affect how well you burn that fuel. Although many of the factors affecting your metabolic rate can't be changed, there are ways to increase the metabolism you were born with. Exercise is at the top of the list for metabolism boosters, with aerobic workouts burning more calories in the short term and weight training that builds muscle and fires up your metabolism in the long run.

Therefore, maximizing your workouts to take advantage of both strategies will help you balance your caloric intake and your weight. Even small bouts of movement give a boost to your metabolic rate, but the following power suggestions will really help make a difference.

- **Add some variety.** Although it's important to engage in a mode of activity that you personally enjoy, there is considerable evidence regarding the benefits of cross-training and adding variety to your workouts. Try out several fitness activities that use different muscle groups than you normally do each week to keep things interesting.

- **Aim for the hills.** Increase the vertical incline at which you move your body, to make your body overcome the demands imposed by gravity. It's one of the most effective ways to increase how hard your body has to work while exercising.

- **Exercise longer and farther.** One of the simplest ways of challenging your body is to extend the duration of your exercise session. The longer you work out and the greater the distance, the more calorie burning and cardiovascular benefits.

- **Lift more.** Progressive overload is the best way to develop your muscular fitness. By placing a demand on your muscles beyond a load that they can normally handle, your muscles become stronger. The more lean muscle in your body, the higher your metabolism burns even at rest, so power up your workouts!

- **No leaning allowed.** Avoid having any part of your body resting on exercise machines while working out. Although this may allow you to work out longer, it can dramatically decrease the amount of work your body is actually doing.

- **Interval training.** Do you want a bigger bang for your workout efforts? There is no better way than with high-intensity interval training (HIIT). Your workouts are divided into two speeds—high intensity and rest—which are alternated for a defined period of time. With HITT, you end up consuming more oxygen (compared to a lower intensity activity), which results in an increase in post-exercise burn.

Keep moving and keep pumping for a revved up metabolism! Incorporate exercise into your day-to-day, whether it's quick 10-minute bouts or formalized classes.

Walk This Way

The benefits of walking are numerous: decreased blood pressure, weight control, blood sugar control, bone strengthening, improving balance and coordination, feeling good and looking good!

The beauty about walking is that it can be done by almost anyone, anywhere and everywhere with minimal training and minimal equipment. Walking is much easier to fit into your daily busy routines and it's natural and much easier on the body than many fitness activities. Even if you're unfit, you can start slowly and build up gradually.

- **Make walking an adventure.** Register for a walking competition to push you to the next level. Signing up for local charity races will not only support a good cause, but it will also motivate you to build consistency into your training. Challenge yourself to try longer distances, push yourself to improve on your race times, or even try out a new terrain than what you are used to.

- **Make time to walk it off.** Plan your schedule around taking a walk during breaks, your lunch time, or anytime you think you might need some fresh air and movement. Use it as a stress reliever, along with giving yourself a boost in metabolism, energy, and productivity. Who needs caffeine?

- **Get a group going.** Get support from others by walking together to help you stick with your health and fitness goals for extra motivation and accountability. Make it fun for the whole group by setting goals like a virtual "walk across the states" challenge or have a friendly pedometer competition at your workplace. Simply spread the word and get organized. Walking is always more fun with friends!

- **Pick up the pace.** Is walking really a workout? Absolutely! You can walk your way to better fitness in as little as 30 minutes a day. The faster, farther, and more frequently you walk, the greater the benefits.

- **Learn how to walk.** Maintaining an upright posture is important for maximizing your efforts and preventing injuries: belly in, face forward, and make shorter, faster, stronger, and more efficient steps by rolling off the back of your foot.

- **These shoes were made for walking.** It might just be worth the money for a good pair of walking shoes that support you, feel comfortable, and go the distance. Choose shoes with proper arch support, a firm heel, and thick flexible soles to cushion your feet and absorb shock. Get measured at a sports shoe store for the best fit and for professional advice on which brands suit your needs.

- **Stretch it out.** Before and after walking, take time to stretch your hamstrings, quads, core, and calf muscles as well as hip flexors and shins. Hold each stretch for 30-40 seconds and don't bounce.

Physical activity doesn't have to be complicated. Something as simple as a daily brisk walk can help you live a healthier and more fit life. Walk your way towards better health!

Flexibility & Balance

Grace … it seems almost like an old-fashioned word in today's world. Grace basically breaks down into two practices—flexibility and balance. Both are areas that most women don't spend enough time developing as they focus instead on anything that burns the maximum amount of calories.

As your body ages, your continued ability to function, care for yourself, and live independently are based on these two factors. Both play a vital role in your overall fitness and way you optimize daily movements. Tight muscles may contribute to back pain and difficulty performing simple tasks, such as putting objects into overhead cupboards or bending down. Poor balance is known to increase the risk of falls. Luckily it is very easy to work on both flexibility and balance on your own.

- **Stretch for performance.** Stretching doesn't just feel good; it helps to improve your flexibility, which in turn may improve your athletic performance and decrease your risk of injury. Before and especially after your activity is the best time to loosen up the most utilized muscles.

- **Sign up for results.** You will achieve the best results with consistency and regularity. Take a look at the classes available through your community center, gym, or worksite and sign up for a Feldenkrais (awareness through movement), Alexander technique, tai chi, Pilates, yoga, barre, or any core-strengthening style class.

- **Practice one-sided balance.** Practice exercises that challenge one side of your body at a time so that each side of your body is forced to bear the load independently. This is great for developing your naturally weaker side, and your muscles, especially the core, have to work hard to maintain your balance. Ballet, paddleboat, golf, or racquet sports are some ideas.

- **Motivation for weight loss.** Most everyone is thinking about, if not actively working on, losing a few pounds. Focusing on improving your balance and flexibility is a great wake-up call to understand how harmful extra weight can be to your body. It is tough to stretch or maintain balance poses with extra weight on your body, especially in the abdominal area.

Whatever you choose to try, the key to any stretching and balance program is regularity. Make your flexibility and balance a priority in your fitness routine and enjoy the benefits now and for years to come.

Partner Up

Beyonce or Rihanna may be your favorite gym buddies, but an amped-up playlist may not motivate you the way a real live training companion can. Having a workout partner can motivate you to exercise simply because you know someone is counting on you to show up. Research indicates that 80% of people believe they are more likely to fit in their workouts and stick to their routines if they partner up. Even better, research from the University of Pittsburgh reported that women who exercised with a buddy lost one-third more weight than those who exercised solo.

The fun comes in with the opportunity to socialize and catch up with friends. Training in tandem or in a group makes it less intimidating to join a gym, try a new class, or sign up for a sports league. Why not enroll in that Latin dance class, join that hiking club, and show up for a 6am workout at the gym? Your buddy will be waiting for you!

- **Grab a buddy.** Get your girlfriend time in while you get in your workout. It's the best form of multi-tasking and the extra accountability will help you stick with your program and keep any boredom at bay.

- **Do it for charity.** Need a little extra motivation with your workouts? How about making the world a better place? Whether a 5K walk, marathon run, century bike ride, or triathlon, you can support various charities while working up a sweat and challenging yourself to greater heights. Many organizations even have training groups for added fun and support. Exercise and do good!

- **Join a club.** Whether a fitness club, softball league, climbing gym, biking organization, running group, or a tennis team, exercising is much more fun with others. Work on group goals as you build camaraderie and friendships.

- **Work with a trainer.** They know how to push you hard and can help you achieve ideal results in usually less time than on your own. Also, making a financial commitment provides the added motivation to show up and maximize your efforts.

- **Couple up.** Partners that play together, stay together! Share a passion for fitness with your other half and not only spend quality time with each other, but also improve both your fitness levels and the bond between the two of you.

A fitness partner can encourage, challenge, and pace you. It's all about accountability and results, but the added benefit is that you get an extra dose of fun!

Nature's Calling

Get some green activity into your fitness routine and head outdoors for a great workout. The positive health benefits of contact with nature, especially while engaging in movement, can't be praised enough. The impact on improving social, psychological, and physical health, as well as overall well-being, is tremendous.

Green exercise, defined by activity done in natural environments, tends to be more restorative and exhilarating than indoor exercise. Even in comparison to organized sports like football, basketball, and soccer that can be played outdoors, there is more of a profound effect from moving your body through natural outdoor spaces. As a result, research shows that there tends to be an increase in the frequency, duration, and intensity of activity when performed in nature. Outdoor exercise also makes people happier, less fatigued and angry, more tranquil and relaxed, and gives a longer lasting energy boost. So head outside and stay a while.

- **Get in the water.** You don't even have to get wet to participate in water sports! Paddle-boarding, kayaking, and rowing give you options on the water, along with all of the fun you can have with water activities on rivers, lakes, and oceans.

- **Walk outdoors.** Be like Forrest Gump and keep on walking! Hit the hills for a hike or take a stroll to do your errands. There is nothing more empowering than using your own two feet to take you places—whether to beautiful vistas or even just to the grocery store.

- **Head for the snow.** The snow is not just for skiing. Don't forget about the large variety of activities you can participate in during the winter. Be inspired by the Winter Olympics and try out some snowboarding, skating, cross country skiing, tubing, or even curling.

- **Grab some wheels.** The fastest way to move using your own power is on a bike. Take advantage and get to where you need to go or sightsee your way around new cities and foreign lands on a bike. Whether on a mountain or road bike, tandem, or a beach cruiser, you're sure to have the best view while you work up a sweat.

- **<u>Go play in the dirt.</u>** Your garden is calling your name! Answer its call by digging, bending, and moving your way toward a beautiful landscape of fresh flowers and produce, all while building muscles and burning calories.

So answer the call of the wild and head outside for as much "green" fun as you can. Hands down nature is nurture.

THE POWER OF NOURISH

The food you eat can be either the safest and most powerful form of medicine or the slowest form of poison.

ANNE WIGMORE

Rachel's first grade daughter announced at dinner one day that their class was talking about nutrition and they were supposed to poll their parents as to how many servings of fruits and vegetables they had consumed that day. Rachel discovered she only had two servings while her daughter had 5 servings. It dawned on Rachel that she had made sure that her daughter had healthy meals and snacks, but was not making her own nutrition and health a priority. Now, every night at dinner, the family reports their fruit and veggie count and Rachel is happy to say that she is finally keeping up with her daughter. She also feels much more *energized* with the extra dose of nutrients for her body and *empowered* that she is finally taking better care of herself. "How and what I eat keeps me motivated, energized, and able to be my best self," she says.

Super Food Multi-Taskers

Do you want the maximum benefit for minimal effort? Multi-task your diet by choosing super foods that not only promote your health, your mood, and your well-being, but may also benefit your weight. Superfoods contain high amounts of various nutrients. They are rich in antioxidants, phytochemicals, vitamins, and minerals that are absorbed more efficiently and provide some serious disease prevention protection. We are talking about the rock stars of quality nutrition!

Superfoods taste good and are easy to incorporate into your meals.

- **Berries–nature's powerhouse.** Blueberries, strawberries, raspberries and blackberries all pack an incredible amount of nutritional goodness into their little packaging. They are loaded with antioxidants and phytonutrients, so don't just look for them in the summer. Make them a year round part of your diet.

- **Bean me up.** Beans are an ideal complex carbohydrate choice. They pack a nutritious punch as a low-fat source of protein, have varied nutrients and high fiber content, and they are low on the glycemic index for long-lasting satiety.

- **Go nuts.** Nuts are rich in heart healthy fats, fiber, plant protein, and antioxidants. Choose raw or dry-roasted almonds, walnuts, cashews, and pistachios. Remember to keep portions moderate for all the benefits without the dense calories.

- **Get your greens.** Dark green leafy veggies like kale, spinach, turnip greens, and collards are power houses of beta carotene, vitamin C, and folic acid.

- **Go whole with grains.** Although quinoa is a powerhouse grain because of its protein content, don't shy away from incorporating other whole grains into your diet. Choose brown rice, whole wheat, barley, oatmeal, buckwheat, wild rice, spelt, amaranth, and millet for the best nutritional and fiber values.

- **It's tea time!** Both green and black teas are high in antioxidants and they give a boost to your metabolism.

- **Think orange.** Whether it's sweet potatoes, yams, carrots, or any other orange fruits and veggies, get ready for a boost of carotenoids that protect you from carcinogens and protect the health of your vision.

- **Go fishing.** Seafood is packed with healthy fats, especially the heart-protective omega-3s found in salmon, mackerel, and sardines.

- **Dark chocolate!** You heard us right. Not only can it be a divine treat, but dark chocolate is high in protective nutrients and is good for your heart and your mood.

So eat to enjoy and eat for your health.

Energize Your Day

Are you looking for a healthy dose of energy that can get you through your entire day—and doesn't involve downing another cup of coffee or grabbing that candy bar?

Going for quick fixes and not being prepared to make healthy choices leaves you grabbing for whatever is in your environment, and that usually means packaged, chemical laden, high sugar, high fat, and processed foods. Not quite the fuel of champions and not what you need for peak performance! Being prepared and choosing fresh foods that contain fiber and protein at every meal and snack will get you on the way to stabilizing your blood sugar and sustaining your focus.

- **Rise and shine.** Study after study demonstrates that breakfast is by far the most important meal of the day for weight control and optimal energy. It doesn't need to be a large meal, but giving your body some nutrition will help end the overnight fast.

- **Mini-meal your day.** Most people need to eat every three to four hours to keep their blood sugars even, allowing for more focus and stable energy levels. Make sure each meal and snack contains fiber and protein and is calorie controlled.

- **Plan a light dinner.** Eating lighter as the day progresses really makes it easier to digest your food and ensures a better night of sleep. Try eating your last bite two hours before bedtime for optimal digestion and a more restful sleep.

- **Protein power.** Make sure to get a minimum of six to seven grams of protein at each meal, including snacks. This can be found in 1-oz meat (chicken, fish, poultry, red meat), ½ cup legumes (black beans, edamame, chickpeas (hummus), 1 cup dairy (milk, yogurt) 1-oz nuts, seeds and cheese, and in many vegetarian alternatives (soy based).

- **Nibble wisely.** A light snack such a ½ PB&J or a protein shake can go a long way in boosting your energy. Think of your snack as the "bridge" between meals to prevent drops in blood sugar so you don't arrive at your next meal ravenously hungry (which inevitably leads to overeating).

- **Hydrate for energy.** When you just can't stop yawning, head for the water cooler before you head for the cafeteria. Staying well-hydrated helps you avoid being drowsy. Always keep a refillable bottle on hand to start sipping when the afternoon slump sets in.

- **Keep a snack stash.** On Mondays, bring in all of your favorite healthy snacks for the week: low-fat Greek yogurts, apples, protein bars, raw nuts, dried fruit, natural peanut butter & whole grain crackers, trail mix, oatmeal packets, cheese sticks, and baby carrots.

Saying "no" to the goodies in the lunch room and staying away from the coffee shop around the corner just got a whole lot easier—no crashing required!

Think Your Drink

Your organs and all vital systems require water in order to function properly. Dehydration can cause various bodily systems to slow down, making you to feel sluggish, fatigued and irritable. The key is to drink fluids **before** you feel thirsty. If you notice that you feel thirsty, it means your body is already slightly dehydrated and is trying to signal to you that it needs hydration. Noticing if your urine color is a light straw color versus a darker more opaque color will let you know if you are drinking enough water for your body's needs.

Keep in mind that you will have increased hydration needs when exercising, while pregnant and breastfeeding, and if you live in a hot climate. The good news is that produce with high fluid content, like watermelon, also contributes to providing your body with the hydration it needs.

- **Eight is great.** Drinking the infamous eight 8-oz glasses of water each day is an easy way to keeping your body working optimally. Keep a reusable water bottle at your desk and a Brita pitcher in the fridge at work. Set a goal to finish a whole Brita by the end of the workday.

- **Break for water.** Take breaks to walk to the water cooler, refill your bottle, and catch up on the office gossip. It's great for socialization, movement, and a focus break—all while getting a little pick-me-up for your body.

- **Avoid desserts in a glass.** Sugary sodas and high calorie juices and smoothies often have more calories than a decadent piece of chocolate cake! Most of them contain six to ten teaspoons of white sugar per serving. Sodas leach phosphorous from our bones, have no nutritional value, and the calories add up without satisfying our hunger or leaving us feeling full.

- **Java Lo Down.** Limit your coffee intake to no more than two cups per day or about 400 mg of caffeine. Even though caffeine studies show improved mental focus and athletic endurance, prevention of Alzheimer's, diabetes, cancer and depression, it still also remains a fact that too much coffee is related to insomnia, restlessness, excitement, tachycardia, tremors, and rapid emptying. Caffeine only works in moderation.

- **Are diet sodas all that?** The answer would be a resounding NO! Drinking diet sodas on empty stomachs produce negative insulin responses and have been shown to increase weight as a result. The research is also unclear on the long-term effects of artificial sweeteners. So stay away or at least minimize your consumption for now.

- **Herbal essence.** Herbal teas are a great way to warm up in the winter and refresh with ice in the summer. Red passion fruit and mint tea make wonderful afternoon breaks. Up to 3 cups of green tea per day contain catechins, which can stop oxidative damage to cells and have been shown to reduce risk of several cancers and even improve blood lipids.

- **Cocktail hour.** Drink no more than one serving of alcohol per day: for women that is five ounces of wine, one (12 ounce) beer, or 1.5 oz of hard (80% proof) liquor.

For a little more kick and flavor add lemon or a sprig of fresh mint or cucumber to your water.

Mindful Eating

Mindful eating is all about being in the present, slowing down, and taking the time to enjoy the meal that is right in front of you. If you eat most of your meals in non-optimal settings (in the car, at your desk, while on the phone—or worse, not at all), this is a sign that you're not engaging all of your senses to create an eating experience. Food becomes functional and just another task to get through your day. Savoring a meal at a leisurely pace is one of life's greatest pleasures, and you lose connection with your food and body if you eat with lots of distractions.

Mindfulness incorporates slowing down and lets you become aware of your feeling of hunger and fullness. You are also able to be more thoughtful with the foods you choose to consume and be present as you eat so that you don't overeat. Mindful eating helps you hear what your body is telling you and how best to nourish it.

- **Slow it down.** Experts say that it takes about 15-20 minutes for your stomach to send your brain the message that it's full, so eating more slowly prevents overeating. Today, eat one meal free of all distractions. Try to eat slowly, enjoying the unique flavors and textures of each bite. If you typically rush through lunch at your desk, go out and enjoy lunch with a co-worker or friend.

- **Know your numbers.** Gage your hunger using a scale based from 1-10. This simple pause to determine the number that best fits both your hunger level and your fullness level will get you in touch with what your body really needs. Rating your hunger at a 1 means you could eat a horse and rating it a 10 means you are so stuffed you cannot comfortably move. Ideally you should start eating at 3 or 4 and stop eating at a 6 or 7.

- **Chew on this.** Chewing foods ad infinitum used to be a form of dieting back in the 1800s. Though this was an extreme form of dieting, today we actually need to make sure we have enough time to chew our food properly! Chewing is where the breakdown of starches begins, and chewing well means you are breaking down the food to be easily digested. Count your chews. Make sure to get five to ten chews per bite.

- **Put the fork down.** Place your fork down on the table between bites and then pick it up again. This will allow more time to chew, converse, and mindfully eat your meal. You might even notice that you are satisfied with far less food with this added pause.

- **Focus your senses.** Pay attention to the colors, smells, textures, flavors, temperatures, and even the sounds (crunch!) of your food. Do not eat with the television on. Don't eat and read. Just focus on the sensory experiences, sitting down to appreciate and enjoy what your meals offers you.

Many cultures build relationships around mealtime. It may be the only time in the day where families can reconnect and let the communication and conversations flow. So slow down and bring the joy back into your meals.

The Nutrition Essentials

Women have nutritional needs that are very different than men, and they tend to vary during pregnancy and as we age. Women also require fewer calories than men, so we need to make sure we make our food choices as nutrient dense as possible. Ideally, you should be getting all your basic requirements through food choices, but in reality, supplementation is helpful as a back-up to make sure your body gets what it needs.

Every year, there is more and more promising research demonstrating how optimal nutrient levels can have a significant positive impact on disease prevention and well-being in women.

Power up your plate!

- **Do I need a multi-vitamin?** Women do not need to take multi-vitamins on a regular basis if they are getting enough nutrition through food. If you think you need a multi-vitamin because your diet is sub-optimal, the best recommendation is Women's One A Day. The Women's One A Day 50+ (over age 50) contains less iron, which is specifically geared toward post menopausal women.

- **Strengthen those bones.** Calcium has been shown to promote bone growth and prevent osteoporosis, which affects millions of women, especially after menopause. Getting the recommended 1,000 mg of calcium can be achieved by consuming three cups of high calcium foods a day, namely milk, yogurt, or fortified orange juice. For many, getting enough calcium is a challenge, and a calcium supplement may be necessary.

- **Get your sunshine.** Vitamin D is now in the spotlight as we discover how valuable it is, not just for calcium absorption, but for amazing disease protection. Sunlight is the largest natural source of vitamin D, as it is manufactured in our skin via UV rays. Just getting outside for five to ten minutes daily helps Vitamin D production in your body.

- **Iron (wo)man.** Iron can be the key to keeping your energy levels running high. It's a mineral that's essential for your blood to deliver oxygen to all the cells throughout your body. The best absorbed iron comes from animal sources like red meat, fish, and poultry.

- **Folate to the rescue.** We know that folate is important for women of childbearing age, but research is now showing that maintaining sufficient levels are beneficial for perimenopausal women as well. Focus on foods such as fortified grains, dark green vegetables, and lean animal proteins.

- **Fish it up.** Omega 3's are more than heart healthy—they are anti-inflammatory agents that benefit conditions from arthritis to heart disease. Consume fatty fish like salmon, halibut, sardines, herring, non-white tuna, and anchovies, and fish oil capsules are also an excellent source as recommended by your physician or Registered Dietitian.

Be proactive with your health and discuss your specific needs with your doctor. If a supplement is needed, it's important to get the right amount for your age and medical history.

Carb Conundrum

Carbohydrates, in the form of sugars and starches, are essential for the proper functioning of our bodies. They are our primary source of energy and are particularly important for people who are active. Yet carbohydrates get a bad rap for being thought of as fattening, bloating, and just plain unhealthy.

There is a difference between processed carbohydrates and whole grain carbs. In addition, eating the right amount of carbohydrates is crucial. Low-carb diets can be harmful because there is a minimum amount of carbohydrates your body requires to maintain itself. Your body needs around 40%-60% of calories from carbs in order to achieve optimal health and function.

- **Make carbs complex.** Limit simple carbohydrates like white sugar, white flours, white rice, and white bread. Bulk up on complex carbs such as brown or wild rice, whole wheat pastas, and breads, and whole grains such as barley, quinoa, and farrow. These forms of carbohydrates are full of fiber and keep blood sugar even longer through a slower absorption rate in the body.

- **Happy carbs.** Serotonin is labeled the happy hormone. In humans, serotonin levels can be increased through eating carbohydrates. Why do women need more carbohydrates? They have more serotonin receptors in the brain. This helps answer the question as to why it is so difficult for women to follow a high protein diet- their bodies naturally crave carbohydrates.

- **Get at least 25 grams of fiber a day.** This is a lot of fiber but it can be done! Eat bread or wraps with at least 6 grams of fiber, beans and legumes that contain 6 grams per ½ cup, and fruits and veggies with pulp and skin (apple, pears, berries) that can provide up to 4 grams per serving of fiber. Highest fiber hitters are bran cereals, flax seeds, and legumes such as red or black beans and chick peas. Broccoli, apples with skin, and nuts and seeds contain excellent sources as well.

- **Sugar detox.** Cookies, vending machine candy, and donuts go well with an afternoon cup of Joe. Unfortunately, sweets are one of the worst things to reach for an energy boost. While it may temporarily give you a sugar high and a burst of energy, you are bound to crash just 30 minutes to an hour later ... with even less energy than before and distracted by your cravings for more sugar. Steer clear of the office candy. Just say "No!"

- **Eat natural sugar.** The safest sugars on the market today come from natural sources such as honey, maple syrup, white sugar, or brown sugar. Agave is sweeter than sugar so you may use less but it is still a glucose-fructose combo just like white table sugar. High fructose corn syrup is in so many foods because it is cheap and manufacturers know the more sugar we eat the more we want!

- **Artificial sugars.** Artificial sweeteners may have minimal calories but they also have no nutrition. "Z Sweet," found in pears, melons, and grapes, is naturally absorbed. The jury is still out on Stevia (Truvia). Sucralose (Splenda) may trigger migraines, and Xyletol, a sugar alcohol, is not absorbed and thus may have a laxative effect for some people. Go natural before you have to rely on the artificial stuff (unless advised by your MD).

Carbohydrates are an important part of every woman's diet and should not be skimped. The body needs carbohydrates and choosing the best forms they come in can benefit your short-term and long-term health.

Weight Management

Most women are weight management experts thanks to all the years of experience they have trying different programs and diets. But no medications, quick fixes, and magic bullets have ever worked to both take weight off and keep it off. So we are left with the basics in making gradual changes in our habits and behaviors. Nothing sexy and too interesting about it, but this is what we know truly works for long-term weight management success. Here are the real secrets to weight control based on evidence based scientific research.

- **Grab your pencils.** Taking the time to jot down what you eat is one of the most effective tools for successful weight loss and maintenance. It makes you accountable for your choices and it helps to take the emotions out of eating and focus on the numbers. You don't need to count calories. Instead, focus on positive behaviors like how many serving of fruit and vegetables you consumed or how many glasses of water you drank.

- **Start your day strong.** Don't skip the most important meal of the day. Make breakfast the kick-off to good energy throughout your day. You'll stabilize your blood sugar, feel good about yourself, and have a healthy start to your day. As a result, you'll be more apt to make good choices as the day goes on. Include a lean protein and complex carb at breakfast. For example, a Greek yogurt with fruit or an egg-white omelet with veggies are great choices.

- **Focus on the good stuff.** Nobody gains weight from eating too many fruits and veggies and drinking too much water. Keep your focus on adding in healthy foods versus focusing on foods you have to eliminate. Keeping it positive is effective and fun!

- **Move it to lose it.** Move your body anytime, anywhere, anyplace! Nothing helps burn calories, improve your mood, and feel good as quickly as exercise. It doesn't matter what you do as long as you are doing it frequently and consistently using as many muscle groups as you can for the best calorie burn.

THE 5 POWER HABITS

- **<u>Make every bite count</u>**. Most decadent and rich bites of food end up being around 50 calories a bite. Ask yourself if the bite you are about to take is worth it. Being mindful of what and how much you are consuming helps to avoid emotional overeating.

- **<u>Sign yourself up.</u>** Register for a weight management program designed around making lifestyle changes and that provides individual or group support. Being accountable to someone else is a great motivator in achieving results.

- **<u>Head to the experts.</u>** Getting support from a nutrition expert is the best investment of your time and money. No more wasted time and money on quick fixes! To find an RDN (Registered Dietitian Nutritionist) in your area log onto www.eatright.org and get the results you're looking for.

Losing weight and keeping it off is a dedicated commitment to lifestyle change. Keeping within a healthy weight range decreases the risk of diabetes, high blood pressure, heart disease, osteoarthritis, and even some forms of cancer. Focus on long-term success and you will be living a lifestyle that not only supports maintaining a healthy weight, but also a lifestyle that feels good!

Eating On The Go

From the early morning rush, to grabbing desk lunches, to dinnertime drama as we rush our kids to their commitments, eating on the go seems to be the way of the world compared to the sit-down meals of our childhood. You may not be able to rearrange your schedule and life, but you can be prepared to fuel well on the fly. Get ready to make fast food work for you and say "no" to sugary snacks because you are armed with something better!

Sometimes the simplest strategies can help you get through busy times with the energy you need. With a little planning, you can make healthy choices even if you're crunched for time.

- **Pre-plan & pre-pack.** You never know what life is going to throw into your schedule, so plan for chaos and be prepared with non-perishable foods like raw nuts, whole grain crackers, and cereal you can keep in your car, work desk, and purse. Then arm yourself daily with fresh snacks you can prep in a jiffy and that are ready to grab and go such as washed grapes, baby carrots, cherry tomatoes, cut up cucumbers, apples, and celery.

- **Fast food doesn't have to mean fried food!** At the airport, while commuting, having a quick meal with the kids—sometimes there just isn't a convenient alternative to fast food places. Make it work for you by opting for whatever is grilled, steamed, roasted, or baked and modify for the extra add-ons and condiments.

- **Make a meal at the market.** Create a meal from the supermarket without much prep time. Healthy options include rotisserie chicken, lean turkey from the deli, bagged salads, fruit, and healthy lines of frozen meals when in a pinch.

- **Stretch your dinners.** Taco Night can be made into a Layered Taco Salad. Grilled chicken can be sliced into a Cesar salad or wrap. Steak can be added to arugula or made into a steak sandwich. Make your healthy dinner meals go the extra mile and save yourself the time and energy of figuring out your lunch meal.

- **Go old-school with your lunches.** Assemble five sandwiches using ten pieces of bread for the week. The following fillings freeze well. 1. Peanut butter & jelly—add banana or apple slices later 2. Deli meat—turkey, ham, roast beef or chicken 3. Cheese—add perishables like tomatoes, lettuce or other fixings before eating.

- **The morning grab and go.** Maximize the start to your day with foods you prepped the night before so you can head out the door with a burst of energy instead of an empty stomach. Wraps with various fillings are great options. As are quickly blended protein shakes with added healthy ingredients.

Our society is on the go more than ever, whether in the car, on a plane or at our work desks. Fight the challenges with strategies and preparation to make eating on the go work for you!

Eat Clean

Get ready to revamp your diet and start eating clean! This means avoiding processed and refined foods that are filled with added salt, fat, sugar, and chemicals. Eating clean helps prevent diseases, generally results in losing weight and just plain feels good for most people.

When you eat whole and fresh, you're choosing foods that provide a bounty of essential nutrients and protection from the lifestyle diseases we face in our lives today. Avoiding artificial ingredients keeps your cells strong and your body systems working efficiently—and if you feel good, you're more likely to take care of yourself in other ways.

- **Steer clear of the "Ps".** Processed and packaged—foods with a label. Anything with a label that is a paragraph long and loaded with chemicals and additives you can't pronounce needs to be on the "steer clear" list. So many of these man-made ingredients have not been thoroughly tested for long-term safety. We know that fresh and wholesome food works well for our bodies, so aim for those instead.

- **Clean up your carbs.** We know the drill by now—stay away from the processed grains and choose the nutrient and fiber dense alternative like bran, whole beans, and quinoa. A small amount is all you need for satiety, fullness, and for a dose of healthy nutrients.

- **Spice it up.** Don't believe the hype that healthy food is boring and bland. You don't need added sodium, sugar, and additives to make food interesting. Take advantage of seasoning with herbs and spices that are easy to use and readily available in fresh forms—basil, mint, oregano, rosemary, sage, thyme, cumin, and turmeric to name a few.

- **Go to the source.** Choose whole foods as much as possible. This means foods that are close to their natural state as you can get them. For example, aim for plenty of fresh fruits and vegetables over processed counterparts. If convenience is essential, frozen is always an alternative.

- **Be vegan?** To become vegan means to stop eating all animal products and go purely plant based. That means no meats, eggs or dairy products. Veganism is a lifestyle choice and not just a quick weight loss or trendy diet plan. To benefit from this diet our bodies need more iron, calcium and B12 sources which can come from many plant based protein derivatives like beans, nuts, and tofu-based products.

- **Go organic with the dirty dozen.** Due to pesticides sprayed on fruits and veggies, buy the following fruits and veggies in organic form if you can: apples, grapes, celery, cucumbers, cherry tomatoes, hot peppers, nectarines, peaches, potatoes , spinach, strawberries, sweet bell peppers, kale & collard greens, and summer squash.

What you eat really does have an effect on how you feel. Eating whole foods and avoiding junk foods as part of a clean eating lifestyle can make all the difference in your energy, mood, and your longevity.

Go Green

Food choices don't just affect your personal health, but also the health of the planet. The fast pace of our lives has encouraged the food industry to produce packaged and convenience foods and we have made choosing foods for ease the priority over our health and well-being. Going green is better for you, it keeps you alive longer, it makes you look better, and it feels good to eat well.

Going green means buying fresh fruits and vegetables, organic meats, and dairy products from local sources, as well as decreasing your carbon foot print through making healthier choices.

- **Shop seasonally.** Produce are the freshest and most affordable when they are bought seasonally. In the winter enjoy spinach, kale, arugula, carrots, winter squash, and potatoes. Fruit and veggie varieties in the summer include cucumbers, tomatoes, peppers, snap peas, fresh berries, and melons.

- **Become a locavore.** Do you know how much petroleum your food used up to get to your plate? Buying local foods is not only eating well and fresh, but it's also costing the environment less through a smaller carbon footprint. Buying food locally also enhances well-being, knowing that you have a direct connection to your community and the Earth it sits on.

- **Connect with your food.** Take the time to enjoy the process of going to a farmer's market, bringing the food home, and washing and chopping it. Connect with nature through smell, taste, and touch. Enjoy food for what it represents—nourishment at so many levels.

- **Color your plate.** Aim for five to nine servings of fruits and or veggies per day. Fill over half your plate with produce at every meal in order to crowd out less healthy choices and to fill up on nutrition powerhouses. Get 1 cup of dark greens or oranges daily, such as spinach, kale, arugula, carrots, or sweet potato. Add kale to your soups in the winter and salads in the summer. Opt for fresh fruits or those packed in water. Use fruit as a dessert with a side of vanilla yogurt in the summer or as a delicious sweet crumble in the winter.

- **Mix it up.** Grab a hold of the blending and juicing craze and create a healthy and easy beverage filled with a variety of whole fruits, vegetables, and other nutrients that are good for you body. Favorite blend-ins include kale, bananas, tofu, berries, seeds, and yogurt.

- **Make your snacks green.** They don't have to technically be the color green, but instead choose wholesome options for snacks like edamame, raw nuts and seeds, air-popped popcorn, dried fruit, guacamole, salsa, hummus, natural nut butters, and organic dairy products.

Food is nurturing and should be enjoyed. Food is not the enemy, nor should it be considered good or bad. Food represents sustenance and feeds both your body and soul.

CONCLUSION

So can you really have it all? Our answer is a resounding, "YES." But you have to be the one to define your ALL. You ... not society, your workplace, your partner, or the woman standing next to you. Balancing all that you want out of life requires determining what it is that actually makes you feel successful. What do you value? What are you passionate about? What brings joy into your life?

Enjoy clearing off your current full plate of the things that don't serve a purpose and are not meaningful to you anymore. Knock off the things that are tied to expectations and roles and truly take pleasure in adding back in the self-care that gives you balance, feels good, and leads to a more energized, empowered, and effective life!

We wrote this book to share what we have seen with our clients, learned from research, and what we have experienced ourselves, in order to inspire women to make a shift. What our mothers and grandmothers did for us, we need to do for our daughters and granddaughters. You don't have to be everything to everyone; you just need to be important to yourself and the benefits to others will follow.

You have discovered your health and wellness is your best asset and that the *5 Power Habits* provide actions you can start anytime and anywhere to make self-care a priority in your life. We encourage you to fill your plate with the self care strategies that suit you and your preferences and your lifestyle. To be able to stick to these actions you not only need to be ready for change, but also open to practicing them until they become habits. Becoming physically and mentally fit is a journey and a process that does not happen overnight, but it does lay the groundwork for living a life on your own terms.

To further support you in "having your all," we have set up tools and links on our website and invite you to log on to www.havingyourall.com. Subscribe to our special offerings and discover the other services we offer. We also encourage you to stay connected with us via social media and look forward to joining you to be role models for the next generation. We raise a glass to your health and well-being ... and to Having Your All.

Cheers!

NOTES: References & Bibliography

REFERENCES
CHAPTER 1: Having IT All-Redefined

1. Slaughter, A.M. (2012, July/August). *Why Women Still Can't Have It All*. Retrieved from The Atlantic Magazine website: http://www.theatlantic.com/magazine/archive/2012/07/why-women-still-cant-have-it-all/309020/

2. Hills, R. (2012, February 16). *Having It All*. Retrieved from The Daily Life website: http://www.dailylife.com.au/life-and-love/work-and-money/having-it-all-20120130-1qpcp.html

CHAPTER 2: How Did We Get Here In The First Place?

3. Lewis, K. (2013). *What is a Gender Role?* Retrieved from the Working Moms About: http://www.workingmoms.about.com

4. Smith, K. (2013). *Lives of Women in the early 1800s*. Retrieved from the University of Washington website: staff.washington.edu/cgiacomi/courses/english200/historicalbriefs/women.html

5. Johnson-Lewis, J.W. (2013). *Women and Work in Early America*. Retrieved from the Women History About website: http://womenshistory.about.com/od/worklaborunions/a/early_america.htm

6. Wikepedia. (2013). *Women in the First World War*. Retrieved from the Wikipedia website: http://en.wikipedia.org/wiki/Women_in_the_First_World_War

7. Andelin, H. (1963). *Fascinating Womanhood*. New York, NY: Random House.

8. Warren, C. (1987). *Madwives: Schizophrenic Women of the 1950s*. New Brunswick, NJ: Rutgers University Press.

9. Tartakovsky, M.S. (2012, February 27). *A Glimpse into Marriage Advice From the 1950s*. Retrieved from the Your Tango website: http://www.yourtango.com/experts/john-m-grohol/glimpse-marriage-advice-1950s

NOTES: References & Bibliography

10. Friedan, B. (1963). *The Feminine Mystique*, New York, NY: W.W. Norton and Co.

11. *Depression: Some Astounding Statistics and What your Should Do.* (2007). Retrieved from the SixWise website: http://www.sixwise.com/newsletters/07/08/29/depression-some-astounding-statistics-and-what-you-should-do-if-you-or-a-loved-one-is-confronting-i.htm

12. Williams, K., & Kurina, L.M. (2002). *The Social Structure Stress and Women's Health*, Philadelphia, PA.: Lippincott Williams Company.

13. Livingston, G., & Cohn D. (2010, June 25). *Childless Up Among All Women; Down Among Women with Advanced Degrees.* Retrieved from the Pew Social Trends website: http://www.pewsocialtrends.org/2010/06/25/childlessness-up-among-all-women-down-among-women-with-advanced-degrees

14. Jang, E. (2012, April). *How Do Women Spend Their Time?* Retrieved from the Real Simple website: http://www.realsimple.com/work-life/life-strategies/time-management/spend-time-00100000077167/

15. Pew Research Foundation. (2009, October 1). *Analysis of the American Time Use Survey.* Retrieved from the Pew Social Trends website: http://www.pewsocialtrends.org/2009/10/01/the-harried-life-of-the-working-mother/

16. U.S. Department of Labor, Bureau of Labor Statistics. (2012). *Employment and Earnings.* Washington DC: U.S. Government Printing Office.

17. Jayson, S. (2012, June 13). *Stress Levels Increase since 1983 New Analysis Shows.* Retrieved from the USA Today website: http://usatoday30.usatoday.com/news/health/story

BIBLIOGRAPHY

Sandeen, B. (unknown). *The "Golden Era?" A Look at the 1950s.* McCalls. Retrieved from the California Lutheran University website: http://www.callutheran.edu/hmc/pages/menu.html

NOTES: References & Bibliography

Wojtczak, H. (2003). *Women of Victorian Sussex: Their Occupations and Dealings with the Law. 1830-1870*. Hastings Press, UK

CHAPTER 3: The "Exhausted" Woman

18. Spar, D. (2013). *Why Women Should Stop Trying to Be Perfect*. Retrieved from the Newsweek website: http://mag.newsweek.com/2012/09/23/why-women-should-stop-trying-to-be-perfect.html

19. Wood, J. (2011). *Gendered Lives: Communication, Gender and Culture.* Independence , KY: Wadsworth/Cengage.

20. Williams, R.B. (2011, September 3). *Good Looks Will Get You That Job, Promotion and Raise. Wired For Success*. Retrieved from Psychology Today website: http://www.psychologytoday.com/blog/wired-success/201109/good-looks-will-get-you-job-promotion-and-raise

21. Pipher, M. (1994). *Reviving Ophelia, Saving the Selves of Adolescent Girls*. New York, NY.: Random House Inc.

22. Barber, N. (2013, May 2). *The Human Beast*. Retrieved from the Psychology Today website: http://www.psychologytoday.com/blog/the-human-beast/201305/why-women-feel-bad-about-their-appearance

23. Mandel,D. (2010). *Addicted to Stress, A Woman's 7 Step Program to Reclaim Joy and Spontaneity in Life*. San Francisco, CA: Jossey-Bass.

BIBLIOGRAPHY

Bianchi, S. M., Robinson J.P., & Milkie, M.A. (2006). *Changing Rhythms of American Family Life*. ASA Rose Series. New York: Russell Sage.

Sharkey, K. (2012, February 29). *Exhausted? Yeah. Isn't Everyone?* Retrieved from the Women's Health magazine website: http://www.womenshealthmag.com/health/so-tired

Strasser-Kauffman, K., et al.(2003, April 24). *Beyond Superwoman: Twenty-Five Top CEO's show Us How To Get a Life*. Cedarville, CA.: Carmel Publishing Company.

NOTES: References & Bibliography

CHAPTER 4: Should We Lean In, Lean Out, Or Just Stay In Bed?

24. Brady, K. (2013, October 21). *Why Are Modern Women So Exhausted?* Retrieved from Women's Health website: http://www.womenshealthmag.com/health/exhaustion

25. Dube, R. (2013, May 9). *Pinterest Stress Afflicts Nearly Half Moms.* Retrieved from today website; http://www.today.com/moms/pinterest-stress-afflicts-nearly-half-moms-survey-says-1C9850275

26. Ford, C. (2013, April 11). *Why You Can Have It All is This Century's Dumbest Question.* Retrieved from the Daily Life website: http://www.dailylife.com.au/news-and-views/dl-opinion/why-can-you-have-it-all-is-this-centurys-dumbest-question-20130411-2hnqg.html

27. Sandberg, S. (2013). *Lean In: Women, Work and the Will to Lead.* New York, NY.: Alfred A Knopf, of Random House.

BIBLIOGRAPHY

Gutierrez, C.M. (2013, March 26). *The Joy of Having To Work: How the Burden of Having To Support My Family Sets Me Free.* Elle Magazine, pp312-16,371.

Warner, J. (2013, August 7). *The Opt-Out Generation Wants Back In.* Retrieved from New York Times Magazine website: http://www.nytimes.com/2013/08/11/magazine/the-opt-out-generation-wants-back-in.html?_r=0

CHAPTER 5: Stress 9-5 And Beyond

28. Stevenson, B., & Wolfers, J. (2009, August). "The Paradox of Declining Female Happiness," *American Economic Journal: Economic Policy*, American Economic Association, vol. 1(2), pages 190-225.

29. Glynn, K., MacLean ,H., Forte ,T., & Cohen, M. (2009, February). "The Association Between Role Overload and Women's Mental Health," *Journal of Women's Health*, 18(2): 217-223. doi:10.1089/jwh.2007.0783

NOTES: References & Bibliography

30. Lombardo, M., et al. (1988, Spring). "Explanation of Success and Derailment in Upper-Level Management Positions," *Journal of Business and Psychology*, Vol 2 (3).

31. Tulgan, B., & Wenk-Somaz, H. (2003). *Performance Under Pressure: Managing Stress in the Workplace*. Amherst, MA.: HRD Press.

32. US Department of Health and Human Services. (2011, February 2). "Stress and Your Health: Frequently Asked Questions," *The National Women's Health Information Center*. Retrieved from the womenshealth.gov website: http://womenshealth.gov/publications/our-publications/fact-sheet/stress-your-health.cfm

33. Weber, L., & Shellenbarger, S. (2013, March). *Office Stress: His vs. Hers*. Retrieved from the Wall Street Journal Health and Wellness website: http://online.wsj.com/news/articles/SB10001424127887324678604578340332290414820

34. American Psychological Association Practice Organization. (2010). PsychologicallyHealthyWorkplaceProgramFactSheet:BytheNumbers. Retrieved from the American Psychological website: http://www.phwa.org/dl/2010phwp_fact_sheet.pdf

35. Hewellt, S.A. (2002, April). *Executive Women and The Myth of Having It All*. Retrieved from the Harvard Business Review website: http://hbr.org/2002/04/executive-women-and-the-myth-of-having-it-all/ar/1

36. *2013 Work and Well-Being Survey*, (2013, March). Retrieved from the America Psychological Association website: http://www.apaexcellence.org/assets/general/2013-work-and-wellbeing-survey-results.pdf

37. Freedman, D. (2012, June). *The Perfected Self*. Retrieved from The Atlantic website: http://www.theatlantic.com/magazine/archive/2012/06/the-perfected-self/308970

38. Ashkenas, R. (2012, October19). *Forget Work-Life Balance: It's Time for Work-Life Blend*. Retrieved from the Forbes website: *http://www.forbes.com/sites/ronashkenas/2012/10/19/forget-work-life-balance-its-time-for-work-life-blend/*

NOTES: References & Bibliography

BIBLIOGRAPHY

Smith, N. (2012, March 28). *Employees Reveal How Stress Affects Their Jobs*. Retrieved from the Business News Daily website: http://www.businessnewsdaily.com/2267-workplace-stress-health-epidemic-perventable-employee-assistance-programs.html

CHAPTER 6: The "Evolved" Woman

39. Tugend, A. (2013, July 14). *A call for a movement to redefine the successful life*. The Retrieved from the New York Times website: http://www.nytimes.com/2013/06/15/your-money/a-call-for-a-movement-to-redefine-the-successful-life.html?_r=0&pagewanted=print

40. The Philips Work Life Survey. (2013, September 11). *More Americans Pursuing Meaning Over Money At Work, Survey Finds*. Retrieved from The Huffington Post website: http://www.huffingtonpost.com/2013/09/11/at-work-more-americans-pu_n_3906976.html

41. Pew Research: Social & Demographic Trends. (2009, October 1). *The Harried Life of The Working Mother*. Retrieved from the Pew Research website: http://www.pewsocialtrends.org/2009/10/01/the-harried-life-of-the-working-mother

42. Barsch, J. (2011, April). *Unlocking the Full Potential of Women in the US Economy*. Retrieved from the McKinsey website:

http://www.mckinsey.com/client_service/organization/latest_thinking/unlocking_the_full_potential

43. Zeno Group PR. (2013, June 21). *Millennial Women Don't Want Top Jobs*. Retrieved from the hyphen website: http://www.hyphen.com/smart-thinking/blog/industry-insight-june-2013.aspx

BIBLIOGRAPHY

Gross, S.T. (2012, July 5). *The New Millennial Values*. Retrieved from the Forbes website: http://www.forbes.com/sites/prospernow/2012/07/05/the-new-millennial-values/ accessed November 2, 2013.

NOTES: References & Bibliography

The Third Metric/Live. (May 19, 2013). *Arianna Huffington's Smith College Commencement Speech On "Redefining Success: The Third Metric"*. Retrieved from the Huffington Post website: http://www.huffingtonpost.com/2013/05/19/arianna-huffington-smith-college-commencement-speech_n_3299888.html

CHAPTER 7: Define Your Values/Define Your Success

44. Sprinkler, P. (2004). *Meditations for Women Who Do Too Much*. New York, NY: Harper Collins.

CHAPTER 8: Living With Passion

45. St. John, R. (2012). *The Power of Passion*. Retrieved from the Ted Talk website: http://ed.ted.com/on/C8O5iIDt

CHAPTER 9: Choose Happy

46. Buckingham, M. (2009, September). *What's Happening to Women's Happiness?* Retrieved from The Huffington Post website: http://www.huffingtonpost.com/marcus-buckingham/whats-happening-to-womens_b_289511.htmlAccessed October 29, 2013

47. Schwartz, B. (2004). *The Paradox of Multiple Choice: Why More Is Less*. New York, NY: HarperCollins.

48. Lybuomirsky, S. (2013). *The Myths of Happiness: What Should Make You Happy But Doesn't, What Shouldn't Make You Happy But Does*. The Penguin Group (USA).

49. O'Callaghan, T. (2010, February). What Makes Women Happy? Retrieved from the Time website: http://healthland.time.com/2010/02/03/what-makes-women-happy/

50. Rettner, R. (2010, May). *Happiness Comes with Age*. Retrieved from the Live Science website: http://www.livescience.com/6444-happiness-age-study-reveals.html

NOTES: References & Bibliography

51. Rubin, G. (2009). *The Happiness Project: Or Why I Spent a Year Trying to Sing in the Morning, Clean my Closets, Fight Right, Read Aristotle and Generally Have More Fun.* Harper, NewYork, NY.

BIBLIOGRAPHY

Bindley, K. (2011, December). *Working Moms Happier Than Stay-At-Home Moms, Study Finds.* Retrieved from the Huffington Post website: http://www.huffingtonpost.com/2011/12/15/study-working-moms-are-ha_n_1152202.html

The Bloomberg Report. (2012, February). *Employee Happiness Matters More Than You Think.* (Retrieved from the Bloomberg Businessweek website: http://www.businessweek.com/debateroom/archives/2012/02/employee_happiness_matters_more_than_you_think.html

Stevenson, B., & Wolfers J. (2009). *The Paradox of Declining Female Happiness*, data from the United States General Social Survey (GSS). Retrieved from the National Bureau of Economic Research website: http://www.nber.org/papers/w14969

Tam, M. (2013). *The Happiness Choice: The Five Decisions That Will Take You From Where You Are to Where You Want to Go.* Hoboken, NJ: John Wiley & Sons.

CHAPTER 10: Success Through Self-Care

52. Ruderman, M. (2013, October 29). *Career Conversations—Controlling Your Destiny: Recognizing Themes, Making Choices.* The Creative Leadership Institute, Hosted by HBA , Webinar 12-1pm ET.

53. Martin, C. (2008, January). The Art of Self-Care. Retrieved from the Experience Life website: http://experiencelife.com/article/the-art-of-self-care/

54. Bellisle, F. (1999, September). "Food Choice, Appetite and Physical Activity." *Public Health Nutr.* ;2(3A):357-61.

NOTES: References & Bibliography

BIBLIOGRAPHY

Richardson, C. (2009). *The Art of Extreme Self-Care: Transform Your Life One Month at a Time.* Carlsbad, CA: Hay House.

CHAPTER 11: No More Excuses

55. Mindtools. (2013). *The Urgent/Important Matrix: Using Time Effectively not Just Efficiently.* Retrieved from the Mindtools website: http://www.mindtools.com/pages/article/newHTE_91.htm

CHAPTER 12: Get Your Groove On

56. DeLong, T.J. (2011*). Flying Without a Net: Turn Fear of Change into Fuel of Success.* Boston, MA.: Harvard Business School Publishing.

57. Duhigg, C. (2012). *The Power of Habit: Why We Do What We Do in Life and Business.* New York, NY: Random House.

58. Metcalfe L., Lohman, T., & Going, S. (2001, May/June). Postmenopausal Women and Exercise for Prevention of Osteoporosis, The Bone Estrogen, Strength Training (BEST) Study. *ACSM Health and Fitness Journal.* 5(3):6‐14.

59. Selk, J. (2013, April 15). *Habit Formation: The 21-Day Myth.* Retrieved from the Forbes website: http://www.forbes.com/sites/jasonselk/2013/04/15/habit-formation-the-21-day-myth

60. Graybeil, A. (2013, January 14). *Exploring the Brain's Relationship to Habits.* Retrieved from the National Science Foundation website: http://www.nsf.gov/discoveries/disc_summ.jsp?org=NSF&cntn_id=126567&preview=false

61. Wing, R. (2009, May 1). *Weight Loss Competitions Produce Encouraging Results.* Retrieved from the Brown news website: News.brown.edu/pressreleases/2009/05/obesity

NOTES: References & Bibliography

CHAPTER 13: Get Ready, Mindset, Go!

62. Greenberg, M.H. (2007). "Optimistic Managers and Their Influence on Productivity & Employee Engagement in a Technology Organization." *University of Pennsylvania Gallup Management Journal*, 2007: Study cited by Robinson, J. online at *It Pays to be Optimistic*, 2007: http://businessjournal.gallup.com/content

63. McKinley, J. (2013, February 26). *Want to Change the World? Be Resilient*. Retrieved from the HBR Blog Network website: http://blogs.hbr.org/2013/02/want-to-change-the-world-be-resilient/

BIBLIOGRAPHY

Woods, H. (2001). *Stepping Up to Power: The Political Journal of American Women*. New York, NY: Basic Books.

CHAPTER 14: It's Time To Power Up!

64. Brehony, K.A. (1996). *Awakening at Midlife*. New York, NY:, Riverhead Books.

POWER HABIT BIBLIOGRAPHY

POWER HABIT 1 - Purpose

Barseghian, T. (2013, February). *How to Foster Grit , Tenacity and Perseverance: An Educators Guide*. Retrieved from the Mind Shift blog: http://blogs.kqed.org/mindshift/2013/02/how-to-foster-grit-tenacity-and-perseverance-an-educators-guide

Beck, M. (2001). *Finding Your Own North Star: Claiming the Life Your Were Meant To Live*. New York, NY: Three Rivers Press.

Buckingham, M. (2009). *Find Your Strongest Life, What the Happiest and Most Successful Women Do Differently*. Nashville TN: Thomas Nelson Inc.

NOTES: References & Bibliography

Carson, S. (2010). *Your Creative Brain, Seven Steps to Maximize Imagination, Productivity and Innovation in Your Life.* San Francisco, CA. Jossey-Bass books.

Csikszentmihalyi , M. (1996). *Creativity, Flow and the Psychology of Discovery and Invention.* New York, NY: HarperCollins.

Csikszentmihalyi ,M. (1990). *Flow.* New York, NY: HarperCollins.

Frankel, L. (2004). *Nice Girls Don't Get the Corner Office, 101 Unconscious Mistakes Women Make That Sabotage Their Careers.* New York, NY. The Warner Book Group

Hseih, T. (2010). *Delivering Happiness, A path to profits, passion and purpose.* New York, NY: Hachette Book Group.

Rath, T. (2007). *Strengthsfinder2.0.* New York, NY: Gallup Press.

Scannell, E. (1996). *Big Book of Business Games.* New York, NY: McGraw-Hill.

Seligman, M. (2011). *Flourish, A Visionary New Understanding of Happiness and Well-being.* New York, NY: Free Press.

Stoddard, A. (2002). *Choosing Happiness, Keys to a Joyful Life.* New York, NY: HarperCollins Publishers.

Tracy, B. (2007). *Eat That Frog, 21 Great Ways to Stop Procrastinating and Get More Done In Life.* San Francisco, CA: Berrett-Koehler Publishers, Inc.

Ware, B. (2012). *Top Five Regrets of The Dying.* USA, Hay House.

Weiss-Numeroff, G. (2013). *Centenarians in America, Their Secrets to Living a Long Vibrant Life.* Victoria BC Canada, Agio Publishing House.

Wesiberg, R. (1993). *Creativity, Beyond the Myth of Genius.* New York, NY: W.H. Freeman and Company.

Winch, G. (2013, November/December). "The Seven Habits of Emotionally Intelligent People." *Psychology Today.* pp.47-48.

NOTES: References & Bibliography

Young, S. (2002). *Great Failures of the Extremely Successful: Mistakes, Adversity, Failure and Other Stepping Stones to Success.* Los Angeles, CA : Tallfellow Press Inc.,

POWER HABIT 2 - Balance

Allen, D. (2001). *Getting Things Done, The Art of Stress Free Productivity.* New York, NY: Penguin Group.

Beaupre Gillespie, B., & Schwartz Temple, H. (2011). *Good Enough is The New Perfect. Finding Happiness and Success in Modern Motherhood*, Ontario, Canada: Harlequin Enterprises Limited.

Brown, B. (2012). *Daring Greatly.* New York, NY: Penguin Group (USA) Inc.

Carroll, M. (2004). *Awake At Work, 35 Practical Buddhist Principles for Discovering Clarity and Balance in the Midst of Work's Chaos.* Boston, MA: Shambhala Publications Inc.

Cranfield, J., Hansen, M., Hewitt, L. (2011). *The Power of Focus, How To Hit Your Business, personal and Financial Targets with Confidence and Certainty.* Deerfield Beach, FL: Health Communications, Inc.

Loehr, J.,& Schwartz T. (2003). *The Power of Full Engagement, managing Energy, Not Time, Is the Key o High Performance and Personal Renewal.* New York, NY: The Free Press.

Morgenstern, J. (2004). *Organizing from the Inside Out, Second edition: The Foolproof System for Organizing Your Home, Your Office and Your Life.* New York, NY: Henry Holt and Company.

Turkle, S. (2011). *Alone Together, Why We Expect More From Technology and Less From each Other.* New York, NY: Basic Books.

Williams M., & Penmann, D. (2011). *Mindfulness: An Eight Week Plan for Finding Peace in a Frantic World.* New York, NY: Rodale Inc.

NOTES: References & Bibliography

POWER HABIT 3- Move

Brogan, C. (2011, October). *106 Excuses That Prevent You From Ever Becoming Great: How to feel good-or at least stop feeling bad,"* Retrieved from the Chris Brogan website: www. chrisbrogan.com.

Dold, K. (2011, June 17). *Fun Workout: Team Up.* Retrieved from the Women's Health website: http://www.womenshealthmag.com/fitness/partner-workout.

Driver, J. (2013, November 19). HITT High Intensity Interval Training Explained. Kindle Edition.

Fogel, A. (2010). *Green Exercise.* Retrieved from Psychology Today website: http://www.psychologytoday.com/blog/body-sense/201009/green-exercise.

Grindod, D., et al. (2006). Six Minute Walk Distance is Greater When Performed In a Group Than Alone. Br J Sports Med;40:876-877.

Harvard Medical School Special Health Report. *Exercise: A Program You Can Live With.* Boston MA: Harvard Press.

Sibold, J.S., & Berg, K. (2009, May 29). *Just 20 minutes of Exercise Can Boost Our Mood for the Next 12 Hours. Presented at the* Am College Sports Medicine Conference 2009.

Oz, M. (2012, September 12). *Goal Power.* Retrieved from the Time Magazine website: http://content.time.com/time/magazine/article/0,9171,2123797,00.html.

POWER HABIT 4- Rejuvenation

Beck, M. (2003). *The Joy Diet: 10 Daily Practices for a Happier Life*, New York, NY: Crown Publishers.

Becker-Phelps, L. (2011, March 23). Stop Unwanted Habits By Learning to Accept Them. Retrieved from the Psychology Today Website: http://www.psychologytoday.com/blog/making-change.

NOTES: References & Bibliography

McClellan, S., & Hamilton, B. (2010). *So Stressed: The Ultimate Stress-relief Plan for Women.* New York, NY: Free Press.

Shrand, J., & Devine, L. (2012). *Manage Your Stress: Overcoming Stress in the Modern World.* New York, NY: St. Martin's Press.

Walsleben, J. (2000). *A Woman's Guide To Sleep.* New York, NY: Three Rivers Press.

POWER HABIT 5- Nourish

Albers, S. (2011, August 17). Mindfully Eating-2nd Edition. Centers of Disease Control (CDC) and Prevention. *Rethink Your Drink.* Retrieved from the CDC website: http://www.cdc.gov/healthyweight/healthy_eating/drinks.html.

Bauer, J. (2007). *Food Cures, Treat Common Health Concerns, Look Younger and Live Longer.* New York, NY: Rodale Inc.

Clark, N. (2013). *Nancy Clark's Sports Nutrition Guidebook-5th Edition.* Champaign Il. Human Kinetics Publisher.

Environmental Working Group. (2013). *Dirty Dozen.* Retrieved from the environmental working group website: http://www.ewg.org/foodnews.

Geagan, K. (2009). *Eat Green Go Lean : Trim Your Waistline with the Ultimate Low-Carbon Footprint*, New York, NY: Rodale Inc.

Grotto, D. (2011). 101 Foods That Could Save Your Life. New York, NY: Bantam Books.

Harvard Women's Health Watch. (2013, January). *The Truth About Dietary Supplements from the January 2013 Harvard Women's Health Watch.* Retrieved from the health Harvard website: http://www.health.harvard.edu/press_releases/the-truth-about-dietary-supplements

Jakubowicz, D., et al. (2013, July 2). *High Calorie Intake at Breakfast vs Dinner Differentially Influences Weight Loss of Overweight and Obese Women.* J. Obesity.

NOTES: References & Bibliography

Mandala Research, LLC. (2011, August) Living Social Dining Out Survey Key Findings. Retrieved from the Mandala Research website: http://mandalaresearch.com/index.php/purchase-reports/view_document/24-livingsocial-dining-out-survey-key-findings.

Tribole, E., & Resch, E. (2003). *Intuitive Eating, A Revolutionary Program That Works.* New York, NY: St Martin's Press.

Wright, J., & Johnson-Larsen, L. (2012). *Eating Clean For Dummies.* Retrieved from the dummies website: http://www.dummies.com/how-to/content/eating-clean-for-dummies-cheat-sheet.html.

Zied, E. (2009). Nutrition at Your Fingertips. New York, NY: The Penguin Group.

EMMA FOGT

Emma Fogt MBA, MS, RDN, FAND is an international speaker and consultant on work life, leadership, wellbeing and health. Trained at Harvard's Brigham and Women's Dietetic Internship, Emma's past 25 years in wellness include nutrition support, obesity research, college teaching, food industry marketing & consulting and clinical pediatric nutrition. She holds a Masters of Science in Nutrition and Communications and a Masters of Business in Healthcare Administration.

Emma has written a children's book called *Lainy Ladybug Tries New Foods*, NCES 2014, has been featured in *Today's Dietitian* and written several research articles and presentations for T*he Academy of Nutrition & Dietetics*. She has written a chapter in *The Geriatric Nutrition Handbook* and appears regularly in the media as a nutrition expert. Emma lives in Pennsylvania with her two children, husband and labradoodle. When not working, Emma practices yoga, paints, cooks, entertains and travels.

NISHA SHAH

Nisha R. Shah, MPH, RDN, is an international health and lifestyle consultant, speaker, blogger, and founder of the lifestyle brand, *Urban Serenity*. Her expertise is in creating a life of optimal health and well-being that supports increased corporate and self-productivity. She has over 20 years of experience working with high-profile professionals, top executives, professional athletes, and concierge medicine private clients. In addition, she provides training and presentation services to various corporate, academic, non-profit, and health organizations.

Nisha graduated from the University of California, Irvine and earned her Masters of Public Health from Loma Linda University. She is a fitness professional with credentials from the American College of Sports Medicine and holds certifications in Stress Management, Holistic Stress Management, Executive Coaching, and Corporate Wellness. She currently works out of San Francisco, Seattle, and Los Angeles.

Nisha has received many honors for her leadership and volunteer work. She is a lifelong student, passionate about literature and the arts, is an avid sportswoman and yogini, and is working on speaking her 5th language so she has more reasons to travel. As a business owner and mother of two, Nisha understands how important self-care and balance are for her personal and professional health, productivity, and well-being.

BOOK YOUR CUSTOMIZED EVENT TODAY:

Keynotes, Workshops, Webinars

HavingYourAll.com

For more information on the book and related wellness programs for corporate, education and non-profit organizations, please e-mail us at
info@havingyourall.com

www.ingramcontent.com/pod-product-compliance
Lightning Source LLC
Chambersburg PA
CBHW071709160426
43195CB00012B/1629